# RIVERS OF DREAMS

# RIVERS OF DREAMS

## Fly Fishing Stories

ROBERT LYON, *editor*

Orca Book Publishers

**Canadian Cataloguing in Publication Data**

Rivers of dreams

ISBN 0–920501–74–5

1. Short stories, Canadian (English).*    2. Canadian fiction (English) — 20th century.*    3. Fly fishing — Fiction.    I. Lyon, Robert, 1947–

PS8323.F59R5 1992    C813'.01083527991    PR9197.35.F59R5 1992
C92–091215–X

Publication assistance provided by the Canada Council.

Cover design by Susan Fergusson

Cover photograph by Randall S. Stetzer

Interior illustrations by Ian Forbes

Printed and bound in Canada

**Orca Book Publishers Ltd.**
P.O. Box 5626,  Station B
Victoria, BC,  Canada
V8R 6S4

To my boys, Brook and Cody

# Aknowledgements:

"To Know a River" from *A River Never Sleeps*, Roderick Haig-Brown, published in 1974 by Douglas & McIntyre (Canadian rights); and from *Return to the River*, published by Lyons and Burford (American rights). Reprinted by permission.

"Salmon through the Hourglass" by Art Lee first appeared in *The Atlantic Salmon Journal*. Reprinted by permission of the author.

"Grimsa Journal" by Nick Lyons originally appeared in *Fly Fisherman* magazine. Reprinted by permission of the author.

"The River Dwight" by J.H. Hall originally appeared in *TriQuarterly*, a publication of Northwestern University.

"Going Fishing" from *Going Fishing* by Negley Farson, published in 1943 by Harcourt Brace and Company.

"Deschutes Journal" by Robert Lyon originally appeared in *Trout* magazine, Fall 1991. Reprinted by permission of the author.

"The Beaverkill" from *Fisherman's Summer*, Roderick Haig-Brown, published by Douglas & McIntyre (Canadian rights), and by Lyons and Burford (American rights). Reprinted by permission.

"Fishing in Hemingway Country" by Jerry Dennis originally appeared in *The New York Times, July, 1989*. Reprinted by permission of the author.

"Salmon, Cider and Oranges" by Randolph Osman. Portions of this article originally appeared in *American Angler and Flytyer* magazine, Spring 1990. Reprinted by permission of the author.

"The Platforms of Despair" from *Death of a Riverkeeper* by Ernest Schweibert, published in 1980 by E.P. Dutton. Reprinted by permission of the author.

"Fish are Such Liars" by Roland Pertwee from *Reading from Pleasure* published in 1957 by Harper.

"The Tongariro" from *Tales of the Angler's Eldorado* by Zane Grey, published in 1926 by Harper Brothers. Reprinted by permission.

## Editor's Note:

I want to thank everyone who submitted material for this book. Whether or not it was ultimately chosen for the collection, it was exciting to have received the flood of manuscripts that showed up in the mail. Most of it was honestly imaginative work, some of it was good by any literary standards, but more importantly perhaps, the sheer abundance of it speaks to the intimate bedfellows fly fishing and literature have become.

Coyote was fishing. Jumping along the river boulders, he managed to corral a salmon. Just as tooth was piercing scale, the fish spoke.

"Wait! what are you doing?"

"This is how it is. Eating is done in this manner. I am going to eat you," laughed Coyote.

"I am an extraordinary fish. A magic fish. I warn you. If you persist in eating me, you will soon see the world as I do."

"What do you see, Salmon? Bubbles? Bits of things rushing past you in the current?" Coyote laughed and swallowed the magic fish.

After awhile Coyote sat down to rest, and the watery essence of the world began to swim around him. He understood that water is the common language. Water is spoken everywhere. He heard a creek harden and grow into a glacier, while snow whispered ice talk. He heard the singing of bright rivers polishing dark mountains, making sand with ceaselessly rippling tongues, while in the sky, vast spinning vapor dragons sang the curling cloud language.

Coyote understood that the fluid expression of the common language is a combination of still, deep, eloquent phrases and wild, polluted, muddy slang.

Just as cruel gossip returns to haunt us, toxic unpronounceable chemical words are seeping through the aquifer haunting the groundwater and spooking the ocean. Coyote realized that if the habitat of water was poisoned, then life herself would soon dry up and become an arid ghost.

Coyote became angry and sad, and the tidal pull of his inner sea was strong. He howled and wept wet tears. He overflowed and washed himself away in a flood. He carved his own arroyo and pooled up like coyote sediment. Half of him evaporated. Half of him was drawn up microscopic root channels into the circulatory system of a ponderosa pine tree. After awhile he was transformed from a liquid into a solid, and Coyote became part of the fragrance of a shining pine needle. After awhile someone cut down and burned the tree, and Coyote steamed out in the smoke and dispersed throughout the atmosphere.

The people who claim to know about such things say that you are breathing in tiny coyote droplets right now.

*Terry Yazzolino, storyteller*

# Contents

∫ ∫ ∫

# Foreword

Share Zane Gray's passion for the Tongariro — "My comrades talked volubly on the way back to camp, but I was silent. I did not feel my heavy wet waders or my leaden boots. The after glow of sunset lingered in the west, faint gold and red over the bold black range. I heard a late bird sing. The roar of the river floated up at intervals. Tongariro!" From Schwiebert, of the Aroy: "The wild torrents are the secret of the river. The flow of the river is fierce, its bottom is filled with stones the size of oranges and cannon balls and grapefruits — and over thousands and thousands of years, only the strongest and largest fish could build their redds and spawn successfully." Rivers like dreams, and rivers that are: "Meanwhile the river itself performed magnificently. It produced a steady hatch of flies throughout the morning — the only indoor mayfly hatch in America, perhaps the world. Fish were rising over the river's entire sinuous course. By folding it like ribbon candy, I had fit nearly two hundred yards of river into my building." J.H. Hall, *The River Dwight.*

Through the following pages flow a dozen or so different rivers, each of which lived with passion in the soul of the fisherman who wrote of it. Stories from the desks of American and Canadian authors: Schwiebert, Haig-Brown, Lee, Grey, Boyanowski, Lyons, and others; rivers from around the world: Spain, North America, Iceland, Norway, New Zealand and

France. You'll find some good reading here; some new, some classic, some obscure. Our objective with this book was to provide a volume of stories that combined a high degree of literary quality and a freshness of perspective with an underlying motif of fly fishing rivers. Those were the guidelines. This is the result.

You'll find one of Schwiebert's best, and one of Lyon's very human pieces about an Icelandic river. Haig-Brown is with us, as is Art Lee, and Jerry Dennis. Thematically, the story that strays furthest from the river theme, I suppose, is the one of a wise old French trout (Roland Pertwee's "Fish are Such Liars" appeared in an old Bennet Cerf collection) but it is so genuinely refreshing and so graciously written that I have chosen to revive it once again (and after all, where does a wise old French trout live, anyway?). Jerry Dennis' "Fishing in Hemingway Country" backlights the title of this book, and Negley Farson puts us back on a fine Chilean river, the Laja, near the middle of the century. Art Lee recreates the salmon camp ambience of the Restigouche and Matapedia rivers in Atlantic Canada. There are other less well known voices too: J.H. Hall's gives us his ingenious man-made river, "The River Dwight," and Gary Watts's "Middle Fork Madness," that speaks to madness as much as fishing. There is Randy Osman's journey to a Spanish river and the internationally known fly tier Bellarmino Martinez, and, finally, my own account of a guide's life on the Deschutes.

You will not find "how to" or "where to" stories here. I'm afraid, as my brother once complained to me of my own writing, that the actual mechanics of fishing are of secondary interest in this work. While the theme of the collection is unquestionably fly fishing and the practice of catch-and-release is a prevailing ethic, I have chosen to include the very occasional piece reflecting different values. The concept of "kill" is not soft-sold in either the Haig-Brown or Farson selection. They do not "keep" fish, as we say today, but quite honestly "kill" them.

Why *River of Dreams*? Because the best of them run down the beds of our hearts and souls as well as between two clay or gravel banks. Some we may have never seen, but only read about. Others we have fished long and hard and know like the backs of our hands. About this same time last year I sent Bob

Tyrrell of Orca Book Publishers a juvenile fishing manuscript of mine. He didn't want the story, it turned out, but responded with an offer to compile and edit this book.

At first, I had to question my own qualifications for this project. There are so many other angling writers who are streamside names and fish around the world, lecturing and promoting the sport. By comparison I live a reclusive life in the San Juan Islands where there is only the mother of all rivers; actual rivers, even streams, there ain't. That spoke to the "dream" part of the title, though, I figured; I fish a lot in my mind. And as "rivers" go, it was a job of mine, a life actually, guiding fly fishermen on one river for a number of years. I know that river well. We would sleep out under the stars in the canyon for four or five days in a row, from the end of May well through the frosts of October. We would float the river in MacKenzie-style river-dories, negotiating rapids that represented a very real danger. I am supremely thankful for this period in my life, for the realm of personal and environmental discoveries it afforded me, and for the intensity of camaraderie it fostered. I had a habit those days of sleeping as close to the water as possible, or even in the drift-boat (to try and absorb the flowingness by sheer juxtaposition, I think), and as a result I would get up every so often (*way* too often!), still asleep and anxious to find it flooding around my cot and I would scurry around waking the rest of the party and plucking things from the rising water. Some nights I would sit alone at midnight by the water and meditate. The river was truly both a mentor and metaphor to me, and represented the very first time in my life that I had such complete and sustained passion for what I was doing. To whatever degree my more publicly known brethren in the sport knew rivers in the quantitative sense, or laterally, I knew this *one* straight up and down. Realizing this, I set to work.

Running north along the foot of the Cascade Mountains the Deschutes carves deep into a dry red earth. It is a lonely, arid country away from the river, but a bustling nest of life along its banks and in the water. It was spring in the desert and winter, still, across the mountains where I lived, when I first entered the canyon. The sagebrush was thick with a pungent yellow pollen then (the smell of it has marked me for life) and the river seemed packed with life, bugs and trout and birds; even the water itself has a certain green opacity that smacked of organic matter. Coming to this river in this canyon for me then was like walking through the wardrobe door into Narnia, and the Deschutes itself, running cold and curling, has all the features I've come to look for in the rivers gracing the pages ahead: power, mystery and finesse.

Putting this project to bed now, a year after its conception, I can see all too clearly the many fine rivers and writers I've had, by necessity, to leave out. There are none of the fine Montana rivers here, the Madison, the Yellowstone or the Big Horn; none of the lazy southern streams or the hard run streams of the Rockies, north or south. No mention of the Northwest Territories with streams like the McKenzie and the Yukon. Nothing from Alaska where fishing is an euphemism for catching. And nothing from the British Isles. Hemingway is present by reference. McLean is obvious only by his absence. Nothing from Wulff and O'Connor, Gierarch, Travers or Brooks, Raymond, Chatham and others. This is by way of the apology you'll find at the front of every such collection — "there just wasn't room. . . . I couldn't fit them all. . . . "

Rivers move with purpose, unrelenting and full of the stuff of natural laws and cycles. Regardless of who writes about them, or doesn't. Rivers embody the kind of clarity and zen-simplicity of function that each of us, whether we want to admit it or not, yearn to align with in our own lives. It is as fishermen that we come to know rivers and through knowing rivers that we come to the knowingness of so much more. It was the river, after all, to which Siddhartha retired, and of which Vasudeva said: 'The river knows everything; one can learn everything from it . . . ' and of rivers to which the wise water rat in The Wind in the Willows concurs: 'What it hasn't got is not worth not having, and what it doesn't know is not worth knowing.'


Robert Lyon
Orcas Island
January, 1992

# To Know a River

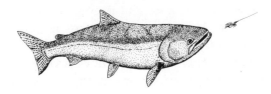

## Roderick Haig-Brown

I have written in this book nearly always of rivers — occasionally of lakes or the salt water, but nearly always of rivers and river fishing. A river is water in its loveliest form; rivers have life and sound and movement and infinity of variation, rivers are veins of the earth through which the life blood returns to the heart. Rivers can attain overwhelming grandeur, as the Columbia does in the reaches all the way from Pasco to the sea; they may slide softly through flat meadows or batter their way down mountain slopes and through narrow canyons; they may be heavy, almost dark, with history, as the Thames is from its mouth at least up to Richmond; or they may be sparkling fresh on mountain slopes through virgin forest and alpine meadows.

Lakes and the sea have great secret depths quite hidden from man and often almost barren of life. A river too may have its deep and secret places, may be so large that one can never know it properly; but most rivers that give sport to fly fishermen are comparatively small, and one feels that it is within the range of the mind to know them intimately — intimately as to their changes through the seasons, as to the shifts and quirks of current, the sharp runs, the slow glides, the eddies and bars and crossing places, the very rocks of the bottom. And in knowing a river intimately is a very large part of the joy of fly fishing.

One may love a river as soon as one sets eyes upon it; it may have certain features that fit instantly with one's conception of beauty, or it may recall the qualities of some other river, well known and deeply loved. One may feel in the same way an instant affinity for a man or a woman and know that here is pleasure and warmth and the foundation of a deep friendship. In either case the full riches of the discovery are not immediately released — they cannot be; only knowledge and close experience can release them. Rivers, I suppose, are not at all like human beings, but it is still possible to make apt comparisons; and this is one: understanding, whether instinctive and immediate or developing naturally through time or grown by conscious effort, is a necessary preliminary to love. Understanding of another human being can never be complete, but as it grows toward completeness, it becomes love almost inevitably. One cannot know intimately all the ways and movements of a river without growing into love of it. And there is no exhaustion to the growth of love through knowledge, whether the love be for a person or a river, because the knowledge can never become complete. One can come to feel in time that the whole is within one's compass, not yet wholly and intimately known, but there for the knowing, within the last little move of reaching; but there will always be something ahead, something more to know.

I have known very few rivers thoroughly and intimately. There is not time to know many, and one can know only certain chosen lengths of the few. I know some miles of the Dorsetshire Frome and of the little river Wrackle that cuts away from the Frome by Stratton Mill and rejoins it farther down, because I grew up with them and had all the quick instinctive learning power of the very young when I fished there. It was a happy and proud thing to know those streams, and the knowing paid great dividends in fish; it paid even greater dividends in something that I can still recapture — sheer happiness in remembering a bend or a run or the spread below a bridge as I saw them best, perhaps open in sunlight with the green weeds trailing and a good fish rising steadily, or perhaps pitted by rain under a gray sky, or white and black and golden, opaque in the long slant of the twilight. I knew those streams through fishing them, through cutting the weeds in them, through shooting ducks and snipe all along them, through setting night lines in them, through exploring them when the hatches were down and the water was very low. I carry them with me wherever I go and can fish them almost as well sitting here as I could were I walking the meadow grass along their banks six thousand miles from here.

I learned other waters almost as easily, though more superficially, when I was very young. The lower reaches of the Frome, between Wool and Wareham, where we used to fish for salmon, were harder to know than the best of the trout water because the river was deeper and darker and slower down there, more secret within itself. But I fished with a man who knew all the secrets, and we used the prawn a lot, fishing it deep down and slow, close to bottom and close under the banks. Fish lay where he said they should lie and took hold as he said they would take, and one remembered and fished it that way for oneself until the knowledge was properly one's own. I think I could still start at Bindon Mill and work on all the way down to the Salmon Water without missing so very many of the good places. And then, perhaps, I could walk back along the railroad track toward evening with a decent weight of salmon on my back.

I knew the little length of narrow carrier in Lewington's field by the bakery at Headbourne Worthy; it was so small and clear that one couldn't help knowing it and so difficult that one had to know it. I knew where each fish lay and why, how he would rise and when, what chance of ground would hide me during the cast, what tuft of grass would probably catch my fly on each attempted recover. And Denis and I knew the narrow part of Avington Lake where the great pike lay under the shadow of the rank weeds; we knew the schools of roach and rudd and the few solitary trout; we had seen the big carp and the slow black trench; we knew, almost, where each little one- or two-pound pike had his hunting ground.

The winter days at Avington, under the tall bare beeches and ashes and sycamores, were very good. There were always mallard to be seen in hundreds, always herons, sometimes a peregrine falcon chasing the mallards; the cock pheasant were richer, burnished gold against the gold of fallen beech leaves, and rabbits sometimes rustled the leaves softly, unaware that we were fishing near them. The rank thick weed banks of the bottom showed clearly, green through the shallow water of the narrow part of the lake. We cast our big spoons and phantoms and wagtails far out, letting them into the unrippled water as gently as we could, then brought them twinkling back over the dark mystery of the weed beds. Sometimes a big pike was lying out over the weeds, and we tried and tried to tempt him. Sometimes one appeared suddenly behind the spoon, followed it and took or turned away. Sometimes — and this was best and surest of all — there was a heavy flash and a swirl as the spoon passed over a known lie, then the pull and the lunging fight.

The first western river I learned was the Nimpkish, the seven twisting miles of it that lie between the lake and the sea. I learned the best of the trout pools first, wading the round and slippery rocks in an old pair of calked shoes, letting the swift water climb up to the pockets of my shirt and sometimes letting it knock me down and carry me half the length of a pool before I could find a way out of it. Then I learned the tyee pools and the cutthroat trout runs of the tidal reaches. Taking the canoe up to go over the traps, lining the big skiff through to the lake, fishing for steelhead, watching the salmon runs, I learned more of it and felt it my own. But I never really knew the river as one can know a river. I don't know, even today, just how and when the steelhead run there, nor more than a fraction of their lying places. And I never could solve the secrets of Ned's Canyon and Wright's Canyon or that third one of the long, slow, deep pools on the river; they were so big, and I knew so many other places to catch fish that it was hard to give them time. But I once wrote a book that had the Nimpkish for a heroine and I saw and learned so much of her for myself through five or six years that I feel my faulty knowledge has given me a full love of her. Whenever I think of a western fishing river, one typical of all the best things that western fishing can offer, I think of the Nimpkish; and I expect I always shall.

The Campbell I know almost as a man should know a river. I don't know the whole story, or anything like the whole story;

but the outlines of plot and characterization are clear and definite, much of the detail is filled in and each new detail fits neatly into an appointed place as I learn it. The Campbell is a little like the Nimpkish, yet most unlike it. Both rivers are broad and clear and swift, with broken, white water, rare, smooth pools and rocky beds. But the Campbell runs only three or four miles to salt water from the foot of its great Elk Falls, beyond which salmon and steelhead and cutthroat trout from the sea cannot pass. The Nimpkish is a highway to all the miles of Nimpkish Lake and the Kla-anche River and Woss Lake, to the Hustan River and the chain of lakes beyond that, and to all the tributary streams of the watershed. The Campbell draws to itself a noble run of winter steelhead, a run of fine cutthroats, a queer little run of small summer steelhead; it has its great tyees, its dying run of humpbacks, a fair run of cohos and dogs in some years, but no more than an occasional sockeye, probably a stray from some other parent stream. The Nimpkish has all the runs that the Campbell has in fullest strength and adds to them a fine run of true summer steelheads, a wonderful sockeye run and a fabulous dog-salmon run. The Campbell is the simpler river of the two, easier to know and understand for all those reasons. Nimpkish is more wonderful, more impressive, more beautiful; but Campbell — and not simply because I live within sight and sound of her — is the better of the two to love.

I can mark the months on the Campbell and tell myself, at least to my own satisfaction, what will be happening in the river during each one of them: In January the steelhead are running well; in February the cutthroats are spawning; in March and April the winter steelheads spawn; in May the little summer steelhead should be in the Island Pools, most of the humpback fry will already have found their way to the sea and the flying ants will hatch out; in August it is time to go to the Canyon Pool and look for the big cutthroats; in September the tyees are in the river; during October the cohos will come; in December the steelhead again. I know the May-fly and stone-fly nymphs that I will find under the rocks and the caddises that will crawl over the bottom in the different months; I know the rocks that the net-winged midges will blacken with their tiny cases, the places where the bright-green cladophora will grow richly, and where and when the rocks will be slippery with brown diatom growth. Some of these things, perhaps, are not important to know if one only wishes to catch fish; but they have their part in the pleasure of fishing.

I find I am quite often wrong about the Campbell even now. I may say that it is too early for the fish to be in, then go up and find them there. I can't always judge when the freshets are coming, but that, perhaps, is no more than saying I'm not an infallible weather prophet. Perhaps it is truer to say that I often find new things about the river than that I am often wrong about her; and sometimes I suddenly realize things that I have known for quite a long time almost unconsciously. It is years, for instance, since I first knew that I could kill fish well in August with the fly I call the "Silver Brown." I tied the fly to imitate coho fry, which are the only numerous salmon fry in that month. In spring, when the river is full of many kinds of fry, the Silver Brown does not do so well for me, and I use the Silver Lady, which has a paler wing and a more complicated tying. I changed over with comparatively little thought, and the true inference of the change only came to me this year — trout may at times feed rather selectively on fry of different species.

Apart from bullheads and sticklebacks, one can expect some five or six different species of fry in the Campbell. Cutthroat fry and coho fry are so much alike that no sensible fish would bother to distinguish between them; it is reasonable to use the Silver Brown as an imitation of both. But humpback fry are like no other fry, trout or salmon; they are, for instance, quite without parr marks, their bellies are brightest silver, their backs generally bluish. I remember that I have fished a fly with long blue hackles for wings and often killed well with it during the humpback run. From there it is only a step to the making of a special humpback imitation; I think I shall start with something of this sort: tail — green swan, body — flat silver tinsel, hackle — scarlet and quite small, wing — blue hackles, back to back, enclosing a white strip and perhaps a strand or two of blue herl, cheeks — pale-blue chatterer. When I fish the river again in springtime, I shall use that fly.

If a coho-cutthroat imitation and a humpback imitation, why not imitations of the others in their days and seasons? The

Silver Lady, perhaps, is sufficiently like spring salmon and steelhead fry. Yet the spring salmon fry has a light brown in his back and an impression of palest pink about him which the steelhead fry has not. It might make all the difference one day. So I shall build a fly with a tail of pink swan, a silver body and wings of barred summer duck enclosing yellow swan; and if that isn't good, I shall try grizzled hackles, preferably from a Plymouth cock with a touch of Red Game in him, set back to back with light-red hackles between them.

None of that is desperately important or highly significant, and I suppose I should feel ashamed of having waited ten or fifteen years to think of it. What I really feel is a good measure of gratitude to the Campbell for having at last brought home to me the rather obvious point that, if it is worth trying for reasonably exact imitations of sedges and May flies, it is worth trying for reasonably exact imitations of salmon and trout fry. In time I shall think of dressings for the green color that is dominant in the backs of dog-salmon fry and the olive-grass green of the young sockeye's back. I may catch very few more fish through my efforts than I should have caught without them, but it's going to be fun.

I fish the Campbell with a sense of ownership fully as strong as that of any legitimate owner of fishing rights in the world, not because I do own any part of the river, nor even because I should like to or should like to keep other people away from it; I should not care to do either of these things. The sense of ownership grows simply from knowing the river. I know the easiest ways along the banks and the best ways down to the pools. I know where to start in at a pool, where to look for the fish in it, how and where I can wade, what point I can reach with an easy cast, what lie I can barely cover with my strongest effort. This is comfortable and pleasant and might well begin to seem monotonous sooner or later were it not something of an illusion. I have a fair idea of what to expect from the river, and usually, because I fish it that way, the river gives me approximately what I expect of it. But sooner or later something always comes up to change the set of my ways. Perhaps one day, waiting for a friend to fish down a pool, I start in a little farther up than usual and immediately hook a fish where I had never been able to hook one before. A little more of the river becomes mine, alive and productive to me. Or perhaps I notice in some unusual slant of light what looks to be a glide of water along the edge of a rapid; I go down to it and work my fly through, and whether or not a fish comes to it, more of the river is known and mine.

For years I have promised myself to fish through the sort of half pool below the Sandy Pool. It starts almost opposite my own line fence and is little more than a smoothing off of the long rapid that runs right down to the Highway Bridge; but there are many big rocks in it and — I can say this now — some obvious holding water. I fished it twice this spring. On the first evening I caught two or three fair-sized cutthroats, and once a really good fish broke water at the fly. I went down earlier on the second evening. A three-pound cutthroat came to my first cast. There was a slow silver glean as the fly came around on the second cast, a solid heavy pull and the 2X gut was broken. I put up heavier gut and hooked a clean steelhead that ran me almost to the end of the backing. I hooked two others along the pool that evening, both of them too close to their spawning; but the pool is the Line Fence Pool now, something so close to home and so obvious that I took ten years to learn about it, a discovery as well worth while as any I have ever made.

One discovers other things than new pools and new fish lies in old pools. One learns to mark one's casts by such things as the kidney stones and the flat rock in General Money's Pool in the Stamp, one learns to hope for the sight of a pileated woodpecker crossing the river in swooping flight at this place, a flock of mergansers at that place, a dipper against black rocks and rippled water somewhere else, deer coming down to eat the moss on the rocks at the water's edge in hard weather. All these things are precious in repetition and, repeated or no, they build the river for one. They are part of the background of knowing and loving it, as is every fish hooked, every cast fished through, every rock trodden. And men and women come strongly into it. Here, I can remind myself, was where Ann sat that first day we came up the river together, and here it was that she loved the September sun the year before Valerie was born. Here we stopped and Letcher made us an old-fashioned before we went on to the Canyon Pool that day. Here Buckie brought his first fish to the bank, here I gaffed Sandy's first steelhead for him, here Tommy hooked one last winter, there it was that the big fish took Reg's line across the roots of the cedar tree. . . .

I still don't know why I fish or why other men fish, except that we like it and it makes us think and feel. But I do know that if it were not for the strong, quick life of rivers, for their sparkle in the sunshine, for the cold grayness of them under rain and the feel of them about my legs as I set my feet hard down on rocks or sand or gravel, I should fish less often. A river is never quite silent; it can never, of its very nature, be quite still; it is never quite the same from one day to the next. It has its own life and its own beauty, and the creatures it nourishes are alive and beautiful also. Perhaps fishing is, for me, only an excuse to be near rivers. If so, I'm glad I thought of it.

# Salmon through the Hourglass

Art Lee

I

If you fail to appreciate understatement, the few remaining traditional Atlantic salmon fishing camps of Quebec's Gaspe Peninsula can be disappointing at first sight — with their seemingly uninspired wood-framed buildings, shingled over and painted white with green trim, white-trimmed-green out-buildings and sheds, a rail fence listing beside a wandering driveway of crushed stone. A dozen rusting cars and pickup trucks are parked helter-skelter not quite out of view. And if anything hints that the peace amounts to more than first meets the eye, it is the new mowed lawn and the fleet of polished station wagons fanned out in the shade of gigantic sugar maples.

Unless it is early morning or evening when you arrive, you'll see no one. The camp looks deserted, the sports in houndstooth jackets present in spirit only. A salmon camp is at rest during the day, its guests and guides away on the river, the staff off stocking up supplies, seeing to family business or napping out of sight. The place won't come to life until shortly before cocktail time when, having returned, the sports and guides will adjourn to their respective places to replay the day's action.

There are those of the opinion that the time of such camps has gone by, that they belong to another era. But others who have been around them long enough will tell you that little has changed at their camps in half a century or more. Everything is as it ought to be, an old guide assures you (as if the fence along the drive had been erected with its present list in mind); everything is *the very best*, because it is the way the sports like it. And that is all that counts.

The camp isn't there to impress outsiders. To those who run it, the outside world might not even exist. Their camp is an insider's thing, exclusively and absolutely, and so they see it somehow as invisible from without.

For years I had watched club members fish the Restigouche River which marks the boundary between the Canadian Provinces of Quebec and New Brunswick, the most storied Atlantic salmon river south of the Gulf of St. Lawrence. Gaspe canoes cut the currents of the river, while sports stood amidships casting first to one side then the other. Such a sight, those slender green boats looking like spears pointing downriver, while the Restigouche sparkled over millions of stones polished by the currents for hundreds, nay, thousands of years. Were I to be among those privileged few, I wondered, could the river and I remain one? Or would that intimacy eventually fade . . . the river no longer a wishing well, the silver salmon tarnished like old coins?

## II

"Good morning, Richard," I greeted the grinning guide who was holding the creaky screen door for me.

"Good morning, sir," Richard Adams replied with a smart little bow. He touched the brim of his hat. Standing on the porch and looking down the pathway toward the Matapedia River, I hoped that this sturdy man in braces and Mountie breeches would get caught up once again in the spirit of the fishing club heydays he no doubt could remember so well.

"I'm glad you spoke out now, Art," said Richard, standing at my shoulder. "You see, if you didn't say something, I wouldn't have opened my mouth. No siree. In those days guides never dared speak a word 'til the sport had broke the ice."

"Then I'm pleased that I said 'good morning'," I said, determined to stick to my role.

"Yessir, my boy, I am too," countered the guide, "or we mighta stood here for a long, long time — like the handsome young lad and the pretty young girl, each waiting for the other to speak out first."

Richard Nelson Adams, it was clear enough, always had the last word these days.

## III

For a week I alternated back and forth between beats on the Restigouche and Matapedia Rivers, thirty miles apart. Each night Richard would join me, my wife, Kris, and our friend Mike Kimball to re-catch salmon that he and his sports had killed years before, when pools now public and overfished seldom saw a fly. Over poached, that is "biled," salmon and rum cokers, Richard recalled the day that "the old man," R.J. Cullan, then president of The International Paper Company, had snatched him off the log boom in the Town of Matapedia and had put him to work as a guide. And he described how once he had ridden two spruce logs like skis down the swollen river for miles, and how he had lugged a female sport on his back across a pool to keep her from losing a salmon to the chute in the tail, and how the sport had later declared the pool to be "Richard's," the name it bears to this day.

Richard cradled the antique salmon rods I had borrowed, twitching the tip of an old split-cane Leonard as though shaking hands with a long-lost friend. With hands as rough as spruce bark, he stroked the Bakelite side-plates of a huge Vom Hofe reel and turning the handle slowly, listened to its click, And then looking up suddenly, he complained that most big salmon that are lost today could be saved if only the sports would use "proper tackle."

Pulling at his braces, Richard re-played all the salmon a young writer could wish for, day by day, pool by pool, fly by fly, pound by pound, over a career that had spanned more than fifty years. There are those who insist that Richard Adams is the greatest Atlantic salmon guide in the world, and if it is so, it is because he is owned by the river and owned by the fish just as surely as a good man is owned by his children.

My customary salmon tackle had been set aside for now — the light rods, new reels, hair-winged flies. My well-worn shirts and soiled swordfish-billed cap also awaited my return from the past. In the meantime, I turned out each morning in bloused trousers, a tweed coat and a necktie when I guessed the weather would stay cool, a summer flannel shirt and poplin jacket when my seat-of-the-pants forecasting decided that the day would get hot.

"All ceremonies are very silly things," or so said Lord Chesterfield many years ago, "Yet a man of the world should know of them." But what did or could I know? This was now and that was then, and by trying to reverse the two, I knew only how hard it could be to predict Gaspe weather, how to somehow keep myself always a little too hot or a little too cold, how to feel just a bit awkward each time I took my seat in the Gaspe canoe, and maybe how to avoid looking too longingly at the informal fishing garb of my fellow anglers.

When you've smoked so many cheap cigars, I concluded after seven days of nostalgia, it is very hard to appreciate a good Habana.

## IV

The fourteen-foot rod that had been such a nuisance to pack turned over the longest line with ease. Standing amidships, my fly swinging in the current, I waved to everybody who stopped on the road to observe me, as no one had ever waved to me when I was the observer. And if someone called out, I answered. And all the time the Restigouche drifted serenely by, seemingly offended no more by my behavior than by the racy jogging shoes worn by Edward Gallant, my guide on that river, I'm sure as a statement of fashion.

My fly was a feathery marriage on a hand-forged, double iron, a Green Highlander that turned with each cast to port and starboard. Its swing was smooth and tight as it was pulled by the river, and I waited expectantly for the swirl that would mark the summit of a salmon's mystical climb from its resting place just off the bottom. When the fish came, it came in a rush and snatched the fly with the synchronized power and delicacy that is sport fishing's ultimate paradox, and when the salmon had the fly and I had the salmon, I could feel it chew on the hook and shake its head in anger.

I heard a cheer from up on the road as the salmon started to run, another when it jumped, all silvery against the deep green of the bank. And at that moment I imagined us, the salmon and me, immortalized in an Ogden Pleissner painting — the sport and his guide in their Gaspe canoe, the sport's long rod arched over the Restigouche, one of her bright salmon leaping and throwing spray to the very feet of the spruce. As Edward poled the boat along to stay abreast of my fish, I believed through every inch of me that all the Restigouche sports and Restigouche guides all the way back to the beginning had paused where they were now in history to long to be at my side.

## V

The salmon was a fine one weighing twenty-eight pounds, a female scooped up into the heavy old net of steel and brass and wood that Richard had loaned me to loan to Edward for my days on the Restigouche. Perhaps a thousand salmon, maybe more, had finished in this net over the years, and that night before dinner Richard had allowed that I had been lucky to kill such a fish with such wonderful tackle. We ate broiled salmon steaks and fiddlehead ferns and I lay on my cot with my boots kicked off, the tie that had bound me all day slung over the nightstand mirror, and we laughed and drank from a bottle of dark rum that Richard had brought up from the village. Good salmon tackle, Richard said, should never be parted with, but should be enjoyed by generation after generation of sports, cared for and handed down like a gold watch or a saddle. His sport that day, he said, had lost a big salmon by using tackle fit only for trout. "'Get yourself a decent reel for the love of God' I told him," said Richard. "They just don't know. He didn't understand. When the salmon's scarce, you hate to lose them."

He said that a poacher had drowned in the Matapedia the night before after going through the chute below Richard's Pool. He shook his head at the greed of the man and the price he had paid for not respecting the salmon or the river. And suddenly, for the first time since I'd known him, the dean of the Matapedia looked very, very tired.

## VI

The three of us walked through a tunnel of spruce to the shore of the Matapedia River. Richard carried my rod and his net, Mike Kimball the paddle and seat cushions.

"When we worked for the club, each sport had two guides," Richard was saying as we reached the canoe. "Not anymore. It would be too dear. But, Mike, you'll do just fine — if you know how to take orders. The bowman's always been the boss, no mistake about that." Richard chuckled, then punched Michael lightly on the shoulder.

"You're the boss, my friend," said Michael. He was having a wonderful time, "If I tried to take over, we'd all drown for sure."

"That's what I like — a man who knows his place. And a rare enough thing it is today, chrissalmighty," said Richard.

Richard noted that Michael really looked the part of a sternman — well-tanned, not too bright, and a little hung over. Richard showed no effects of the night-before's rum and went about instructing sternman and sport as to the ritual for boarding a Gaspe canoe as it had been practiced by guides back in the old days.

Steadying the canoe with his long spruce pole, Richard had Mike take my arm gently and lead me to the canoe's center seat. "The bowman nor sport ever got their feet wet," said Richard while making sure that Michael was in the water at least calf-deep. "The very best," he said finally. "Now go around back and push off . . . and try to come aboard and pick up your pole without knocking Art's bloody head off."

"We'd like to go fishing today, Michael," I said, ducking to avoid the shot I knew I would take as soon as Mike had laid hands on his pole.

"That's it, Mike." Richard winked at me. "Teach the sport a bit of respect . . . but never forget it's him that pays you."

Poling a Gaspe canoe and positioning it correctly above salmon lies are among the little miracles that Richard has performed daily between June and September every season since finding himself a guide. And so despite Michael's dubious assistance, the boat shot upstream against the strong Matapedia currents with Richard applying just enough force by climbing his pole to maintain the course he had chosen. Propped up there in my wicker seat like an emperor or mogul, I couldn't help but feel that somehow it would be more fun to play traditional guide than traditional sport. So to pass the time, I rode my sternman — who was splashing away in an awkward attempt to set and drive his pole in time with Richard's — mercilessly.

"Okay now, Mike, put down your pole and take hold of the anchor line," Richard commanded finally, "and we'll see if we can't find our sport a salmon." Michael obeyed, and with one mighty push of his pole, Richard slid the canoe toward midstream. "Let her down easy now, Michael my boy," ordered Richard, "and tie her off to the cleat."

The canoe couldn't have been better placed had we been sketched to the spot. Before us lay a long wedge of water, tapering downward toward the far bank. The Matapedia boiled over several submerged boulders that broke the current in such a way as to create ideal resting places for traveling salmon. The salmon liked best to lie starting about ten feet off the bank, Richard told me, an easy cast with my big antique rod.

"Try this," said Richard. He offered me a fly. It was one of only two that he carried, and he was certain that it would be *"une mouche veinarde,"* a lucky fly, that afternoon. The fly was an old Black Dose that knew the pool well, he said, which inspired me to fish as hard and as carefully as I've ever fished in my life.

While I was casting, Richard and Michael chattered ceaselessly — something that guides would never have dared do in the old days — acknowledging my presence only now and then with remarks such as how it was a veritable wonder that all the salmon in the Matapedia River weren't leaping into a Gaspe canoe that was carrying two such handsome guides and such an elegant sport.

Late in the afternoon Richard asked for a turn at the rod, and he fished a full drop, making long casts and jigging the rod tip mightily to impart action to the fly. He always moved his fly, he said, to tease the salmon; and he confessed that through the years he had had to hook a lot of fish for his sports.

"They claim it's the casting that tires them out," he said, "but that's not it at all. It's the air of the Matapedia Valley that does it. It's like having your back washed with good lye soap by a pretty girl, good God."

We didn't kill a salmon that afternoon, although the sun was well down before we finally gave it up. Evening mist lay on the river and we dallied on shore to see through a Matapedia nightfall. Richard did some chores around the canoe, and we ate dried meat and sharp cheese and drank from a bottle of water that Richard had filled at the spring that runs behind his riverside cabin.

A doe and twin fawns forged the river at the tail of the pool, and Richard paused to tip his hat. His long white hair spilled over his collar, and his profile might have belonged to a statesman.

"Should we be moving on?" he asked politely.

## VII

"I guided an old feller just a week ago," Richard was saying. "Ninety-two year old, he was. We saved a twenty-pounder at Jim's Rock, raised one and lost another. And the old feller he says to me, 'Richard, I'll be back next year and we'll have our limit before noon.' 'Yessir,' I told him. 'I want to be sure that you'll guide me, Richard,' he says. 'Well, God willing, I surely will, sir,' I told him. You know, boys, he looked at me as if I was ninety-two and he was, well, you know, young like me, and he says, 'You're a good guide, Richard, and you'll be on the Matapedia River for as long as the Good Lord decides to send a salmon.'"

# Grimsa Journal

Nick Lyons

*Sunday Night*: Salmon. There are salmon everywhere: salmon leaping the falls behind the lodge, their force astonishing; salmon and salmon rivers — this year's, last year's — in everyone's talk; smoked and poached salmon on the table; on the wall, old and new photographs of men with notable salmon; salmon statistics in the log, with pool, fly, and size listed; salmon in my dreams.

And at dinner, at eleven o'clock, after the first evening of fishing, almost everyone said they had taken a few. Schwiebert took one ten minutes after we got to the river — a bright six-pounder in one of the lower pools. Dick Talleur said he was no longer "a virgin": he had taken his first, lost a second. Joe Rosch, who had never fished for them, brought back two — one better than twelve pounds. He said his hands and knees were shaking after it was netted; he said that, from the excitement, he had fallen flush into the icy river.

The Grimsa is low but it is filled with salmon. Ten times this afternoon, before we fished, I walked back to the falls, where salmon — some small, some perhaps ten to fifteen pounds — were making their headlong, vital, terrible, exultant leaps at the top of the rush of white water. In the foam and swirl below the falls you could see a tail, a back, flick black out of the white boil. How bright and powerful they are. One four-pounder kept missing the falls and leaping smack into wet lava. I do silly things, too, when caught in the spawning urge.

I have never fished for salmon, but I am catching salmon fever. Perhaps I won't get any. Tonight I was bewildered. I made cast after cast with my #10 rod and double-hooked Blue Charm: across and downstream, then a little half step and another cast across and downstream. Nothing. Nothing whatsoever. The worst of it was that fish were jumping, coming clear of the water and falling back every few minutes. Big fish. Bigger fish than I had ever seen in a river. Sleek, silver, determined fish. I had not a tick. I went back over my beat four times and moved not one fish.

After a spell, inching downriver along the lava and lava-rubble bottom, watching the crystalline water that appears devoid of all life but for the salmon, you begin to think you will never catch one of these fish. There seems so little logic to it. Sparse once told me: "By God, the beggar isn't even feeding when he's in the river. If a fish rises to my fly, I want to know why." I have not the slightest notion how to get these mysterious fish to move. Even the flies have strange names: Blue Charm, Black Fairy, Thunder and Lightning, Hairy Mary, Green Butt, Silver Rat. In sizes #6 to #10, double-hooked. Which to use?

Still, what a lot of fun we have had so far. We got to Reykjavik at nine Saturday morning, slept, and walked through the closed town (except for Talleur, who is training for the Montreal marathon and *ran* a short ten miles). The city, built mostly of concrete, since there are few trees, is quaint, even charming. Woolens, silverwork, and ceramics are the chief wares — and they're very handsome. Then we had dinner at Naust, which Ernest said was the finest restaurant in Iceland.

The place is like an old sailboat, with little round windows and nameplates of old ships at each table. We ate graflax — which is raw salmon treated with herbs, buried in the earth, then served with mustard and brown-sugar sauce — and then the others chose grilled baby lobster tails, an Icelandic specialty; I had British beef and we all drank a lot of wine and then had ice cream and brandy. Ernest told us about the early witch hunts in Iceland, which ended when someone said: "Hey, you fellows are killing off the most interesting girls in town." And

Dan Callaghan told one about a guy who ate a couple of stoneflies, washed them down with a glass of wine, paused, and said, "The wine's not right." Talleur was there, and Bob Dodge (who is paired with me for the week), and Bob Buckmaster, who has read and loved Plunket-Greene's *Where The Bright Waters Meet*, and any man who's liked that book I know I am going to like. Anne and Dick Strain, the Perry Joneses, and Joe Rosch, the others in our party, ate elsewhere. We are from Iowa and Albany, New York City and Bellefontaine, North Carolina and Oregon, and we are all in pursuit of this fish bright from the sea, about which I know less than nothing.

The two-hour bus trip from Reykjavik to the Grimsa Lodge this morning wound past the Hvalfjord, which served as an American naval base during the war, and into the Iceland landscape, which is stark, treeless, and curiously beautiful.

Now it is eleven-thirty and we are settled into the well-appointed lodge that Schwiebert built and there is still light in the sky and I am exhausted. I am also high-keyed, tense. I know this kind of intense fishing. It will be necessary to catch a fish or two before the edge is off. Maybe tomorrow.

*Monday Afternoon*: Got my first salmon late this morning on Beat 3, the Strengir. I had fished hard since seven o'clock, casting across and downstream time after time. Buckmaster had given me a crash course on how to tie and fish the riffle hitch. An interesting technique. Since the fly is visible, the take is more dramatic than when the fly is fished conventionally. After a few hours I tried it and an hour later saw a good fish flash. I held back my impulse to strike, then struck and felt him.

The fish went to the bottom of a heavy riffle, shook its head, and sulked for five minutes. I could not budge it. Then it went a bit upstream, then down into the next pool. And in ten more minutes, Gumi, our ghillie, netted it. I was thrilled to get a first salmon, a seven-pounder, but, except for the force of the thing, disappointed in the fight. It had not jumped. It had not taken me into the backing. "Brown salmon," said Buckmaster at lunch. "He's been in the river too long. They don't eat, you know, and lose something every day." This not-eating inspired me. I wished I could learn how to not-eat for three months at a stretch. But the food at the lodge — heaping plates of lamb, halibut, salmon, potatoes — and irresistible desserts, is too good.

I got another fish soon after the first, about four pounds, then struck a fish bright from the sea. It went off like a firecracker, leaped, got below me, let me get below it, and finally I beached it. A good morning. The edge is off.

Fished with Buckmaster this afternoon. What a lot of fun he is to be with. Peppery. Wise about salmon. Full of stories. We were on a difficult pool called, with good reason, "Horrible." Bob uses only a fly he ties called the Iowa Squirrel Tail, in fairly large sizes, with a riffle hitch, and he was determined to get one. He cast long and with great skill and then riffled the fly into the slick before a falls. Nothing. Then we went upstream with Topy, his ghillie, and the two of them coached me into catching a small sea trout. Bob went back to "Horrible" and worked hard for more than an hour but caught nothing. Still, we'd found a lot to laugh about and the company was awfully good, so the afternoon was a delight. "There's more to fishing than to fish."

"What you're looking for," Schwiebert said, "is a salmon with an itch." I have been looking awfully hard. I don't even know what day it is. My right hand is becoming locked in the casting position, and at night I can feel the thrust of the Grimsa against me and inside me that rhythmic, endless pattern of casting across and downstream, inching forward a half step, then another cast, then watching the fly rise and sweep across with that pretty little "vee." I've caught nothing in several sessions now, and the wind has become raw, snarling. My casting hand is blotched and swollen from sun and wind and a certain lunatic look has come into my eyes.

Anne and Dick Strain invited me to fish with them this afternoon and I did, on the Strengir again. Anne is avidly looking for new species of birds and is a fount of information about them and about the flora. She pointed out the alpine thyme clustered in small patches of bright purple everywhere, cotton grass, yellow hawkweed, and pink thrift. I can recognize the whimbrel, with its long curved bill, and the arctic tern.

Dick took two good fish in the last of the five Strengir runs, then, exhausted from casting my heavy rod into the wind, I lent it to him: whereupon he promptly took a third salmon. I tried for another hour but raised not a fish. Then Sven, their ghillie, came by and I lent him the rod: whereupon he promptly hooked a good salmon. They called it the Lucky Rod. I have begun to wonder if my first three salmon weren't flukes. Will I ever get another?

Fishing intensely, you grow not to see yourself. Ernest told me at lunch that salmon fishing makes manic-depressives of us all. I feel low. Is it because Bob Dodge got such a fine bright fish this morning, then another, while I got none? I hope not. I enjoyed watching him fight that fish for nearly a half hour, then net it. It was about nine pounds and terribly strong, and it jumped and ran and when he finally had it his hands were trembling. We took a dozen photographs of him there on Beat 1, holding the fish by the tail, with the falls and the lodge in the background. His excitement was irrepressible. He went up to the lodge, got some scotch, which we all drank riverside, and said, "If I don't get another fish this week, I'll be satisfied."

But this afternoon I feel low, and it is apparently visible, and I still wonder if I'll ever get another salmon.

More snarling wind and cold but no rain. I got one seven-pound fish, the only salmon of the afternoon by anyone in the party. Is it Tuesday?

Every morning we breakfast, a few at a time, as we get up. A buffet of bread, butter, marmalade, sardines in tomato sauce, cereal, and black coffee is laid out, and we can add two eggs cooked to order with ham or bacon. I always sit facing the window, where I can watch the water and the falls. Fewer salmon are leaping now. We need rain.

Then we rouse our partner, head to the wet room, and put on waders and vest. It is cold in the mornings and I have been wearing a cotton shirt, a Cambrian Flyfisher's sweater, and an ochre guide's shirt; yesterday I had to add a scarf. Everyone else has felt soles on their waders, which hold well on the lava; I wear my cleated soft-aluminum and felt rubbers, which have proved excellent.

Our gear is virtually what you would use for large trout: a rod for an 8 line (which I have switched to from my 10), 18-pound test backing (which no one has needed yet), and a heavy leader, 12-pound test and up. The best flies have been the Blue Charm, Rusty Rat, Colly Dog, and Black Tube, all on a double hook, in the smaller sizes.

You learn to fish the lies, not the rise. You begin to *see* the lies in your dreams as the week progresses and you rotate beats. Fishing until ten, then talking another few hours, then rising early and spending long hours on your feet, everyone gets tired. Joe has started to skip supper. Some of us have skipped part of a morning's fishing, others rest when their turn at "Horrible" comes. Talleur rested by running sixteen miles yesterday.

In the mornings at seven, and then again at four, the ghillies wait outside the wet room. Most of them speak English reasonably well; only Ernest, among us, speaks some Icelandic, which someone told me is not a language but a throat disease.

Each day you learn a bit more. The salmon react in a new way, striking in the lower end of the pool, in the slick; you learn the slow and steady Crossfield retrieve for water without sufficient current to swing the fly, or how to vibrate your rod horizontally to induce a take. You cast a bit better and you learn the virtue of careful casting by the increased interest the fish show when your flies land three inches rather than ten from the far bank. When the salmon roll or jump you think of dry flies — but they won't work here any more than you'll find a mosquito: bad trade. You learn to shorten your leader to seven feet, 16-pound test, against stiff wind, and that this does not bother the fish a whit. When a salmon is on, you have a fish with saltwater size and power in trout-stream conditions, and you remember that Earl West told you to play these fish hard, that a half minute's rest and you have a fresh salmon on again — so you add more pressure and are amazed that you have not yet lost a fish among the five — or is it six? — you've caught so far.

You watch Schwiebert carefully. He is deft, economical, wise about this river. He teaches you the lies and how much skill truly matters. He knows the history of each pool.

And, knowing the river itself more intimately each day, you look forward with greater expectation to the rotation of the beat. You know the beat is better and you have more confidence that you can do this thing. This morning we have Beat 5, which has been fishing extremely well. I think about that as I step out of the wet room and walk with Bob toward Gumi's car.

∫ ∫ ∫

Joe looked shaken tonight. He had lost a big salmon. Very big. He had seen the fish roll just above the falls at the tail of Beat 3 and had tied on a small Blue Charm, cast slightly upstream, mended twice, and watched the huge fish take it solidly. The salmon leaped, raced upriver, settled into the pool, then, after ten minutes, leaped again and headed for the falls. Joe decided to try to turn him and the fly pulled free. Now he thinks he should have let the fish go down the falls; he charted the route and thinks he could have followed it. There was much talk and the consensus was that this would have been wisest. The ghillie thought the fish would have gone twenty pounds, perhaps more.

Joe was shaken but he has caught an unforgettable memory.

I am fishing his beat tomorrow and asked him to map out the spot. Still no rain.

∫ ∫ ∫

An interesting afternoon with Bob Dodge. We fished a long flat stretch the others call "The Lake." Perhaps sixty or more salmon are stacked up here, waiting for higher water, and Dan Callaghan and Perry Jones have taken good fish here. Bob went across stream, inched over to the lip of the bluff, and served as "point man" for me. But I could not, though I cast over the salmon many times, move any of them.

Later we went upriver and each took a good fish in broken water. We are beginning to know a bit more about the river and about salmon fishing, and we have at least some confidence that anyone who can use a fly rod reasonably well can take fish. Iceland is not the moon and salmon fishing is not astro-physics.

A flash of bright silver. The fly turning out of the eddy, buffaloing downstream. The tooled lunge. Up, out of the black near the rock he came, into white water, his back curved and turning. Up and out and then down on the fly as it gained speed and began to zip. I waited. And waited. There! I struck, felt the fish throb, and then he careened off, down toward the rapids. Forty, fifty feet of line. Sixty. The first foot of backing came through my fingers.

Then he stopped, shook his head, started off again, and leaped, smashing the water, shaking, and falling back.

Fifteen minutes later I had him on my side of the river. I looked up and saw a dozen cars lined along the bridge, watching. The salmon jumped again, ten feet from me. Ten minutes later he turned to his side and I led him to shallow water. The fish was ten pounds, bright silver, and bolted off when I disengaged the fly.

It is Thursday.

*Friday Night*: I tailed my first salmon today, a nine-pounder from Beat 5. Dick Talleur was there and got out his camera.

"No!" I called to him, hiding my face. "I've made my reputation by *not* catching fish."

"No one deserves a fish like that more than you, Nicky," he said, "after all your family disasters."

"My reputation . . . "

"I won't blackmail you," he said, clicking off a couple of shots.

When I had gotten a good grip on the salmon's tail, I raised the fish high and kept it high, and kept smiling, long after Dick had stopped shooting.

A little later, upriver, I had four good strikes and could not come up with a fish. Buckmaster kept asking if I was striking too fast. "No," I said, after checking my fly, after discovering that I had busted off both points on the double-hooked fly, "just fishing not wisely but too true to form."

∫ ∫ ∫

Anne Strain has seen and identified twenty-six different birds, including the gyr-falcon, red-necked phalarope, black-tailed godwit, white wagtail, turnstone, merlin, arctic redpoil, and wheatear. I like the names. I should watch the water a bit less, the sky more. It is strangely beautiful here — spare, the meadows in varying shades of green, spotted, white, and brown Icelandic ponies drinking at the river, the gray streaks of lava everywhere, the snow-splotched mountains, the vast Montana-like space, that little red-roofed Lutheran church on the hillside, the neat farms, sheep everywhere, places where you can look up a valley at four, five waterfalls, one over the other, silver in the sunshine, sunsets the color of salmon flesh, and the light, the light that is always here, even late into the night, making the days longer, fuller.

*Sunday Morning*: I am exhausted. We leave for the plane in an hour.

Last night Talleur and Buckmaster asked me to go to a local dance with them. Bob wanted to know more about the people. I realized that all I know of Iceland was Shnorri Sturluson and *Egil's Saga*, read in graduate school, and that the country had 222,000 people, rampant inflation, gorgeous sweaters, and great salmon rivers. We left at one o'clock at night, in a Land Rover packed with young ghillies, the cook, and a couple of pretty girls working at the lodge.

Images: the jammed dancehall and Bob Buckmaster, who is past sixty-five, doing a convincing hustle or rope or robot or whatever it's called; the blinking lights; rock in Icelandic; the young eager faces; Talleur breaking training with a vengeance; the trip back at five in the morning, as the light broke, drinking bitter Brennivin (known locally, and for good reason, as "the black death"), watching thermal geysers and meandering salmon rivers taking the first glints of light, and all singing, at the top of our lungs, in English, "When The Saints Come Marching In."

Then Bob Dodge and I were out at seven, because we had the most productive beat, and I could hardly stand. But I took a good salmon quickly and that seemed a good way to end matters. "Take up your swords," I mumbled, "the morning dew shall rust them," gave my rod to Gumi, and leaned back in the car to dream of the terrible swift strike of the salmon.

Meanwhile, Bob hit into a slew of salmon with an itch, had ten good strikes, missed a few, hooked and lost a few, and took four fish. A better way to end matters.

Now we're packed and ready to leave. It has been a splendid, memorable week. Too brief. Schwiebert and Callaghan caught the most fish, over twenty each, and Anne Strain got a magnificent nineteen-pounder that struck at ten o'clock and fought her until after eleven last night. I got enough.

There is already talk of coming back. The phrase "trip of a lifetime" has been used. There is talk about the effect of this place.

But is Talleur really serious about training on graflax and peanut butter?

# Middle Fork Madness

Gary A. Watt

Squinting to tie some midges, I wonder if fly fishing isn't a very peculiar form of madness. Rubbing my eyes, I lose focus and the Plumas National Forest map tacked to the wall of my shop rushes toward me. Like a reluctant criminal, my eyes return slowly to the scene of the crime. The names roll hauntingly off the tip of my tongue; Little Bear Creek, Deadman Spring, Sherman Bar. Closing my eyes again, I spin through time, emerging feebly into blackness . . .

Anguish returns to me as the spectre rises. The fish that teases, taunts, and drives me crazy is the bulging, bullying brown trout of the Middle Fork of the Feather River.

My map says there is a rough camp at Milsap Bar, and that a road leads there, this road hopefully. Paul is behind us, somewhere. I lose him in the dark, then find him again moments later as his headlights strike my rear-view mirror. Cursing the decision to drive up here at night, I remember that it was mine. The road, and that's a generous label, is washboard hell. The truck suffers unmercifully. The track writhes down into nothing more than wheel imprints with grass grown up in the center, and a wall of fir on each side. My high beams are swallowed by the choking darkness. The light seems afraid to get too far away from the truck. So do I.

Fariba breaks the silence.

"We should wait for Paul." A voice of reason, my wife's.

Paul is typically cool, calculating, and deliberate. He would know if we're on the right trail or not.

"Are we lost?" he shouts as his truck rolls up to ours.

My kidneys can't take going back up the mountain, so we'll keep probing down. There are no points of reference, just mountainous shadows on the one side, abyss on the other. Are we fifty feet from the river, or fifty miles? The road is reborn, finally, and levels out. River smells waft through the cool night air. Water roars underneath a bridge as we crawl over.

Pretending to know we've found Milsap Bar, we erect our base camp. Moths dive-bomb our lantern, but the light remains shy, illuminating very little. The ground rises swiftly away from us in all directions, so we feel quite small. Fariba and I bid good night to Paul. The impression that giants are standing over us hangs heavy as we cling together in the void, drifting off finally into a fitful sleep.

The vacuum of sound is ripped apart by waves of high pitched barking. I murmur that there must be a den of foxes nearby. I hope that's what it is, anyway. I also hope that morning comes soon, releasing us from our dim senses, and their captivity in the black blanket thrown down around us.

Morning light frees us and we're stunned by our surroundings. The giants still hover over us, their faces all granite, their shoulders all bony and bumpy. They're dressed up in a well-worn coat of fir, spruce, pine and alder. Their feet are wrapped in blackberry and willow. Their stony, grim faces offer us a less than enthusiastic welcome. They chastise us for invading their realm.

A gentle, foamy falls drops into an emerald swimming hole, just yards from our tents. A short walk down river and the south branch pours into the true middle fork, near the bridge we crossed last night. Upstream of the bridge is mile after mile of wild and scenic river. My pulse quickens as I survey the landscape. My nerves tingle and my fidgety fingers are anxious to tie on a fly.

The canyon is much too steep for total comfort. Pine and spruce stretch for sunlight, leaning precariously out over the plunging depths. Rockslides and deadfalls rest uncomfortably, as if the angle of repose is about to be overcome violently. To fish the Middle Fork of the Feather is to become a dwarf. Hopping big rocks and looking up into boulders diminishes my stature. My eyes climb the slopes and I get dizzy just as I discover the narrow channel of blue that seems to be just an upside down reflection of the river.

The first major bend is a long, smooth, glassy glide. Wading out into the stream is easy here, facilitated by a carpet of sand. Fariba casts a Humpy, (she always does). I toss a Grizzly Wulff, and Paul, ever the risk taker, selects an Elk Hair Caddis. Watching these flies drift is mesmerizing. They bounce and bobble along, and then they are crushed by reckless rainbow trout! We have discovered a school, they're ravenous, and so we play doubles and triples. I release a foot long fighter and cast again. My excitement is electric, and I wonder that I don't short out in the river. I drool with anticipation for the moment when the Wulff careens around the corner, the river rips open, my hands pulsate and the rod bends again!

The late morning sunlight catches us greedily gorging our senses on these hardy fish. The heat finally cools the fishing, and we retreat. Rivulets of perspiration cling to my brow. Paul leans on a rock, grinning. Fariba mumbles something about Humpy, the wonder fly. Laughter breaks out all around. We've struck it rich on the Feather River!

On rocky recliners we sit around a small amber fire. My eyes trace the black shadows of the mountains, higher and higher, and I'm glad I'm sitting. Arching my neck backward, I finally find a blood red river running over me. The blood turns dark blue, then black, as my eyelids have an avalanche of their own. My muscles go numb as I fall asleep at the feet of the giants.

Death by nibbling is an unpleasant prospect. A brood of German Shepherd young blocks the trail up stream. I count seven and see no Momma dog around. The critters are about six months old, and put up stiff resistance. Behind them, pitched in the sand, is what might have been called a tent in better days. Pots and pans are strewn about and a pick and a shovel rest amongst the litter. Our trail skirts an eight foot drop into ten feet of crystal water. The pack surges forward, the leader going for my boot. My shouts make them retreat a yard or two, but they rally and charge again. We retreat a little, to buy some time. The brutes are not that big, but neither are pirhana!

"Git over heer," a raspy voice cracks out of the mountain.

Paul catches Fariba as her start pitches her out over the edge. I cram my heart back down my throat. The beasts slide over toward the tent, whining nervously. As I stare at the tent, an apparition materializes out of the blackberry thicket which clogs a gulch going straight up the hill. The thing skulks forward, shoeless, black-brown trousers frayed at the bottoms and ripped at the knees. He sports a sleeveless denim shirt, and what might have been a cap makes a crown. The flesh extruding from the openings is a whirl of cracks and folds withered like the bark on a dead tree. A roll-your-own hangs from black lips, while yellow teeth humor us in the fashion of a crooked smirk.

"Folks done sem feshing?" he inquires.

Centuries go by before Paul returns, "Sure, some fly fishing."

The creature's eyes start to glow, tightening down into slits of fire.

"If yer goin' up river, watch fer dem big brownie. Big Goddamn brownie. Maybe you git em. Maybe like dat gold, ya git nothin'!" the ghoul howled.

Aeons skip by and the man-thing and his army of teeth melt back through the thicket. Paul's voice comes down to me through the ages, urging me to move on. Eventually I do, but it's hard to keep from falling down, since I keep looking back over my shoulder.

We fall silent for a spell. The canyon has closed in tight, forcing us to pick our way carefully among the ledges. As we pass Devil's Gulch, the giants press us close, daring us to make one false move.

"I hope Big Brownie doesn't mean the pups' mother or father," Fariba says, "If it does we may be going for a swim."

"Maybe Big Brownie is a bear, or a sasquatch!" Paul chimes in.

"He meant brown trout," I say, the image of the raggedy prospector struck in my head.

A nervous tension sticks to me. Looking up, I see great fluffy schooners sailing over the canyon. The prospect of being caught here on these shelves in a storm, or of being run down by Big Brownie the phantom, leaves my confidence shaken. Maybe it's just the heights, but I feel flattened, like one of the giants has casually tossed a ton of stone down on top of me. I can't wait for the trail to open up again. At least then a person can flee, dodging all manner of monsters, before breaking up on the rocks.

We're working Wooly Worms near Hunters Ravine as the new day begins to warm. Paul spots it first, calling me up. Fariba, playing tug of war with a fourteen inch trout frees herself and trots up a moment later. Big Brownie has shown up.

Near the far bank of the river, small silver streaks explode out of the water, some even landing on the damp, sandy shore. Watching a fish rise to a fly is one spectacle, but witnessing fingerling rainbow trout fling their bodies recklessly into the air is quite another!

Once more Paul sees it first. A dorsal fin juts from the water, a tail fin does the same. A broad back, heavily spotted, splits the stream in two. A silvery body rolls and betrays a subtle golden belly. The prospector's words come back to us all at once, "Big Goddamn brownie!"

The predator slashes through the shallows, silver projectiles blasting off around its mouth. The whopper has cornered the tiny trout in a back bay and indulges in a feeding frenzy. A trophy sized brown, world renowned night feeder, is having brunch before our very eyes.

Paul goes right to the heart of the matter, tying on a Little Rainbow Trout, and easing himself out into midstream. A double haul plops the streamer right into the chaos. My friend lets the offering sink, twitching the fly as it swims through the commotion. I hold my breath, fists clenched, ready for the take. The killer passes near Paul's imitation, chomping down instead on a natural. Several perfect casts go unanswered, then Fariba and I can't hold back any longer.

I select a White Marabou, Fariba tries a Black Nosed Dace. We try everything. Tribute is made to the classic wet flies, the streamers, the beautiful and the ugly. Brief homage is paid to Skues, Hewitt, Sawyer, Leisenring and Brooks. As all goes for naught, and panic sets in, we revert to cruder, sloppier methods.

Finally the missiles subside, and the big fins disappear. The exhibition has lasted some twenty-five minutes, as we feverishly pitch hooks to our exposed fish. Big Brownie is having none of it, frustrating our efforts. We lean our rods against a boulder. The phantom of the deep has deserted us. Fariba scoops up some water and pours it over her head, cooling off. Paul, wide eyed, looks at me in disbelief. I look up at the giants, but they look down in silence, offering no explanation.

∫ ∫ ∫

Two days later we camp near Little Bear Creek. A caddis hatch is coming off, persuading Fariba to abandon the wonder fly for an Elk Hair Caddis. Trout pockmark the river, each way we look. We don't have to be accurate, for if we miss one rise form the fly is shortly intercepted anyway. It isn't a classic duel, fish-hunter stalking elusive lunker, but it is fast, furious and fun!

Our eagle-eyed scout notices a big bulge behind some mid-river boulders. Releasing a red-side, I glance upstream toward the place Paul indicates. The bulge becomes an eruption, a flash of yellow and a very wide tail visible in the breach. Another Middle Fork monster.

Intermittent stones keep fouling Paul's line causing the caddis to wake instead of drift. We search for a place to ford the river, and a chance to cast from the other side. Whitewater up above forces us to go downstream, where we tiptoe across, water tumbling over our hip boots before we can reach the shallow water again.

Deep water forces us to higher ground as we plod back toward our target. Blackberry vines twist, tangle and choke the trail, forcing us to start climbing. I look back across to Fariba, and like a symphony conductor, she is busy orchestrating a series of pirouettes out of a very large rainbow. We're making more vertical progress than horizontal until finally we're stopped by a sandy slide covered in dead leaves and small limbs that the giants have discarded.

I traverse first, Paul follows. I slip first, Paul follows. Sliding down the mountain on my butt, my feet strike a lone tree below me, and I hold fast. My partner zips past me, upright, his arms flailing like a whirling dervish. He misses the tree, shoots out over a drop airborne, bounces once then goes head first into the blackberries below!

Our ordeal ends as we gingerly walk out onto the gravel spit that we once so coveted from the other side. I wave in admiration as Fariba holds up another scarlet prize. I wonder how much time we've wasted bushwhacking, how many fish we could've caught, but suddenly the monster rises, chasing all doubt from my mind.

I motion for Paul to go first, after all he spotted this one. The fish rises once more, and a small wake hits the beach where we stand in awe. Paul waits. The fish rises again. Paul hesitates further.

"What the hell are you waiting for?"

"I'm timing the rises," he calmly informs me.

"Cast the damn fly or get out of my way!" I scream at him in the silence of my mind. I'm stunned. This is no time for scientific investigation. I pace the shore.

Finally, he casts. He mends the line. He rips his rod skyward.

"Fish on!" he shouts.

He doesn't have to tell me. I jump up and down on the sand and gravel, pumping my fists in triumph. Paul's rod bends deeply, the drag ticking reluctantly. The fish swims around a submerged boulder, slaps the surface viciously, then dives again. Paul edges down stream, encouraging the brown to fight the man and the current too. The fish, unfazed by the force of the water, tows nylon upstream, rounds the aquatic rock, turns back toward us and completes the knot. My friend's face goes white with horror.

"Slack line!" I yell madly.

Paul valiantly throws a mend up over the boulder on the third or fourth try. He recovers the slack quickly, bracing for the pull at the other end. It never comes. The brute is already free. The fly is still there, though mangled. The fly line has abrasions from hugging the rock. He looks at me in disgust. I press my hands to my temples, closing my eyes.

"It had to be all of six pounds!" he mourns.

"Closer to eight, I'm sure," I correct.

Recovering by our fire, we relate the highs and lows of our

small adventure to Fariba. Exhausted, as much by our brief encounter with Big Brownie as by our trek, we fall silent once more.

"That must have been quite a fish, Paul," Fariba confides in her soothing, melodic tone.

Paul does not answer. We keep our silence too, listening instead to the chatter of the driftwood in our fire, and gazing up into all the candles in the sky.

In the morning we declare a moratorium on fishing, move our camp up to Deadman Spring, and indulge in a day of rest. Fariba goes swimming, then basks in the sun, brushing her chestnut hair. I pan for gold and find lots, all of it fool's. Paul has disappeared up Dogwood Creek promising to put his photographic skills to work.

The day wears on in timeless summer fashion. Fariba and I play lovers, making small talk and taking turns napping on each other's shoulders. Later, Paul stuns us by returning with a sack full of frogs' legs. We have enough flour and oil left to make a feast, then sit around congratulating ourselves on avoiding most of the moon food in our backpacks. After dinner Paul plays magician again, surprising us with a hat filled with wild strawberries, small in size but huge in flavor. We suggest he go hiking more often!

In spite of our one day prohibition, I start getting anxious to fish again, just as the afternoon starts to die. Sitting around all day plotting strategy, I have formed a plan. I've chosen the head of a large pool, and will wait until dark before casting. A weighted Muddler seems like the perfect probe for the murky depths. As I take up my post in the pool, I can see trout rising in the slicks below me.

Twilight creeps in and still I have not cast. Some mosquitoes enjoy my inactivity, as I stand paralysed in the knee-deep water. Looking over my shoulder I see Fariba and Paul honoring the moratorium, flickering into ghostly proportions behind a roaring fire. I begin to doubt my sanity as huge cups of steaming coffee appear in the shadows all around me. I shake off the cravings and keep my vigil.

Darkness finally subdues light and I cast up and across, mending heavily, purchasing time for my Muddler to dive. The fly weaves this way and that, I mend back and forth, until finally it hangs directly down river. I strip line back in, square myself, and begin again, shooting hard toward the far side. The fly quivers as it sinks. I guide it cautiously, twitching the line occasionally as it swings past me. Somewhere in the blackness below, the fly hangs high, close to the surface. I lift my rod slightly, stripping a couple of feet of line in, beginning the process one more time.

Suddenly the pole is jerked nearly out of my hands! I rear back, setting the hook viciously.

"I got one!" I shout toward my companions.

My unseen opponent tugs hard, my reel squeals for relief. I palm the reel, walking blindly downstream, hoarding the line. A tremendous splash sings to me and ripples of river ride into my knees. The drag whine some more, and I concede what little line I've gained.

The night numbs my sense of proportion, but it seems I've lost most of the pool, and the beast must be dogging the bottom of the tail out slick. Groping about with my feet, I stumble over a submerged log, pitching forward into the water. Thrusting my hands out in front, I clench my teeth, ready for pain. I bubble under, then surface seconds later without my rod! Searching frantically I finally kick the pole, pulling it out of the water just in time to feel a massive surge from the other end. It feels as if the giants have reached down and ripped the fish away from me.

Paul's flashlight beam finds me turned to stone, staring downstream. Retrieving my line, I examine the fly, marvelling at the L-shaped hook. Paul sees it too, his jaw hanging open.

Beside the fire stone turns back into flesh, as hot coffee thaws the blood. I wonder what my nemesis was, but the knot in my gut tells me it was another trophy brown trout.

"Are you in the habit of pitch dark meandering, on these large freestone rivers?" Paul inquires.

"It's a recent vocation," I parry sardonically.

We burst out laughing simultaneously. Fariba pulls my ear, reproaching me for my breakneck tactics. She then kisses me on the cheek, before joining the hysterics. We laugh until we cry, the frustration of several losing battles peeling away. Our laughter echoes out over the river, until it seems like the giants are laughing too. Fiendishly, madly, they bend over howling, slapping their knees. They make sport of us.

∫ ∫ ∫

The next day our arrival at a point just above Sherman Bar is curious. Just as our time is running out, so it seems is our path up river. A hundred-foot high wall blocks our progress. Whitewater makes wading around the blockade impossible. The far side offers only a blackberry jungle. We'll camp here, and start working our way back tomorrow.

The evening hatch isn't caddis, but mayfly. The duns have a soft yellow body, with cloudy wings. We have Pale Evening Duns that are very close in design, and put them to work as the emergence intensifies. The rainbow trout begin to rise in earnest as shadows crawl up the necks of the giants. Fariba and I work some veins of water created by the splitting of the river at a jumble of boulders below a waterfall. Paul stands on a sand bar above the falls, casting into the main arm of the river. We're only beginning when Paul notices a cascade of water erupting on the smooth run that is just out of our reach. He points and I see the fish roll again. I shrug my shoulders, as if to say, "What's the use, if we can't reach it?"

Paul abandons the rainbows, walking over to the base of the wall. I know what he's thinking, and join him. Fariba shakes her head in disbelief as we begin to climb the fortress.

I make it up some forty feet, but want to go no further. Paul is high above me, and seems to find the going easy.

"I'm going back," I holler as Paul disappears into some rusty colored shrubs on top of the rampart.

I'm lamenting my lack of climbing skills, deploring my fear of heights, when I notice some small hand and toe holds going out around the belly of the wall. They're a mere fifteen feet or so above the river, a height that I can deal with, or so I think. What a wizard I'll be when I skirt my way around the abdomen of this stony sentinel, magically greeting Paul as he descends the other side!

This is a big mistake. I make it half way and cling to the navel of the rock. My muscles ache, my legs cramp, and I drool from holding my fly rod in my teeth. I glance down between my legs and see a frothy white river waiting for me to drop in.

I hit the water in a crash, my rod pulling out of my mouth, my hat popping off as I go under. The hat precedes me, while I bounce along the bottom, choking. I go over the small falls and emerge like a crippled nymph, making for the surface. Fariba's hands pull me to shore, where my cap and rod are already resting. I sprawl on my back, wondering if I've lost any vital parts or shed any blood. Providence is with me. I'm chastened, embarrassed, foolish, but lucky, staring up into the pretty face that frowns back. Fariba chides me some for my lack of better judgement, then resumes stalking a rather large riser.

I manage to sit up just in time to see Paul casting at the top of the glide. I resent not being there, then think worse fates, and feeling humbled, fall back on the ground again.

Paul's shouts bring me back to life. I stand in time to see him fighting a huge fish. The trout makes several consecutive jumps, steelhead style, dives, then sails through the air away from Paul. He plays the fish tough, but slowly concedes ground to the fighter. The line points straight towards Fariba and me, and the fish rests just feet from the falls. Tension mounts as a standoff ensues.

The fish suddenly zooms towards Paul, some twenty feet, then reverses course, blasting downstream. Paul, cut off by the very wall he previously scaled, makes his final stand. The line tightens just as the trout hits the waterfall. Boom, its over.

The picture of the fish, all gold with black spots and red dots, sticks in my mind as I watch the tail waters, hoping the prize might be stunned. There is no sign of the brown trout, or of Paul either, until my friend appears at the top of the wall. When he gets to the bottom, Fariba shows him a beautiful sixteen-inch trout, but to Paul, and to me as well, the rainbow seems inconsequential! Night closes in as we light our campfire. Humbled, I need dry clothes. Distressed, Paul needs time to think. Fariba needs only to rest her arms, weary from catching hungry rainbows.

Back at base camp we rest for a day, in the shade of the alders and willows surrounding the swimming hole. Hiking back across the high mountain ridges has been hot, exhausting work. We nurse our wounds, Paul and I having collected more than just a few bruises.

Evening finds Paul scratching an itch that has arisen. Fariba, preferring to rest her laurels as well as her arms, remains cosy by the fire. It's up to me to walk back down the main camp road, and cast a fly into the confluence of the Little North Fork and the main stem.

A few risers show, taking teeny caddis flies. I'm loathe to engage them, but twist on a trusty Elk Hair, and flail away. Over on the side of the confluence pool the surface ruptures as if the giants have dropped a granite basketball on the river. I feverishly redirect my fly to that spot, making several casts before reconsidering my offering.

I switch to a size 10 Cranefly, awkwardly pitching it onto the still waters. I lift the fly away and with no more style than before, slap it back down again. Darkness drops down hard and I can't see the fly any more. I need no eyes to see though, only ears to hear the jaws close and hands to set the hook.

I wait in vain. While mosquitoes do not, my quarry feeds elsewhere. I can see him wreaking havoc below me, striking terror into all the timid tenants of the deep. I can feel his teeth gnashing as he sucks in another victim. I know he grows bigger, while I stand here getting smaller.

Black, furtive figures careen through the air around me. I cast one last time and one of the bats moves to intercept me. Even he prefers the natural though, swerving away at the last second! As the bats become invisible, I feel the hair rise on the back of my neck. The night does not belong to the two-legged creatures and I feel like I should hide behind a rock. I turn back toward camp, feeling my way through the ebony thicket. The bushes along the water make anxious murmurs, telling me to hurry. Finally, the light of the fire, like the fingers on some great bony hand, beckon me toward a safer haven.

$$\int \int \int$$

A voice surprises me from the door. Fariba. Startled, I jump off the bench, wondering how long I've been staring at that map. I look down and see the midge struggling, so I loosen the vise to free it, placing it with the others.

"Hi," she says, smiling.

I look at her over-long, then begin smiling myself. It was all like a dream. Fariba walks over. "Driftin'?"

Coming from a long way back my mind swirls into the present. I dwell on this woman's pretty and contented face, on the wise way it is with women, their secret and special grace, the harmony they have with it all that makes us men look like overgrown children so much of the time. And what better example, it dawns on me then, than the trip.

"I was thinking back on our trip," I tell her.

"That was a wonderful trip, wasn't it?" she says.

"You enjoyed yourself, didn't you?"

"Very much," she says, slipping around and holding me from behind, "but I worry about you and Paul sometimes, you know; you act like men possessed."

"Madness," I mutter.

"Yes, it's very much like that."

"It's a consuming kind of thing."

"Evidently."

"And you know, we look for that, we want it that way, men do. This was Middle Fork madness and although it's a special experience, special place and everything, there's Eel madness and Umpqua madness, even Mad River madness, you know; the list goes on."

"It's something you bring to it, I think, too, don't you? As much as the place itself?"

"Yes, of course."

"Like back on the Middle Fork I had a wonderful time being there in the canyon and fishing for rainbows, but it was a different kind of wonderful, I'm sure, than yours and Paul's."

I turn my head and catch her eye. "Way different," I agree. "Interesting how that is."

"Boys and girls," she says.

"Sure seems like it."

"Boys and girls," she says again, laughing, "*way* definitely."

# The River Dwight

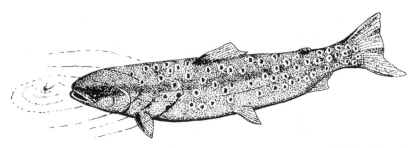

## J.H. Hall

Whenever someone asks me how I got started in the indoor
fishing business, I say it was luck. I don't say if it was good or
bad luck. I let them decide.

I'm a Registered Maine Guide by profession, which is quite
an honor, but as my wife, Marie, liked to remind me, it's not a
paying position unless you actually get out there and take
people hunting and fishing. Well, I don't hunt; so right away I
was at a disadvantage. I fish, but under very strict guidelines —
flies only and no kill — so my clientele was on the small side,
which suited me fine. I was more into research and
development anyway. Marie said what I did was not
"research"; it was reading. She had other words for it too, most
of which you won't find in your thesaurus. Marie's a Licensed
Practical Nurse; she was getting more practical every day.

The fact was, I'd come up with some pretty good ideas over
the years. I held the patents to Dwight's Titanium Rod Tips
(they'll bend, but they will not break) and Dwight's Threaded
Ferrules (no more seized rod sections; no more separations in
mid-cast). With all the four piece travel rods coming on the
market, I saw threaded ferrules as a growth industry, though so
far the manufacturers had missed the boat. I told Marie to try
and look at these patents as annuities. "One day they'll pay off.
You'll see." She said, "Maybe, but in the meantime I'll stick

with the Tri-State Megabucks. Better odds." Marie had lost a lot of faith in me over the years. Maybe we both had.

I did most of my research in the Maine State Library, and it was there I came up with the idea of indoor fishing. But I didn't get it out of books. That day I was tired of reading. My eyes were weary, and I needed a break. I walked over to the window and watched the snow fall. Barely December and we were already into our third storm. As I watched the yellow stains and dog mess disappear, I thought, "Wouldn't it be nice if our lives were like that, if all our mistakes and false starts could be covered over with something white and pure that in the spring would wash away, carrying our miscues with it."

Soon I grew tired of watching snow and thinking big thoughts, so I wandered back through the museum section of the library, 12,000 years of Maine history. The first 11,800 was a tale told in stone. The stones were said to be implements, tools. Each minor modification of rock was supposed to represent some great societal advance, in some cases a whole new culture. To a person with even a speck of imagination, it was a very depressing exhibit. Heck, my threaded ferrules represented a bigger advance in fishing implements than these people had made in ten thousand years. Not meaning any disrespect to Native Americans, but I believe if I had lived in those days, I could have cut — conservatively speaking — centuries off their development.

Next there was a section on Pilgrims and Colonial Life, which everyone who lived in New England was supposed to love, but which bored me more than the rocks, because most of the items — trivets, quilts, and other quaint knickknacks — were still available in catalogues. I say, let it go. Let it die!

Then came the logging and lobstering exhibits, followed by a series of Maine Wildlife Scenes—stuffed animals in their natural habitat, meaning plastic trees and paper maché rocks. At least there was a logic, a consistency of concept that ran unbroken through the beaver bog scene, the salt marsh scene, the moose scene, deer scene, bear scene, but then the concept collapsed. It was shattered by the trout stream scene, because here was movement: water flowing over actual rock into a small pool, at the bottom of which, finning quietly, looking expectantly upstream, were real living fish! Brook trout, char, if you will, whose sleek, lively shapes heaped shame upon all the inanimate exhibits.

This was new; this was stunning. I leaned against the glass and stared longingly at the fish. I wanted to break through the pane and lie down beside the flowing water. I don't know how long I had been there, when I felt a light, bird-like tapping on my back. It startled me; I wheeled around and saw a small, harmless looking, grey-haired lady.

"I'm sorry," she said. "I didn't mean to frighten you, but it's closing time. You wouldn't want to get locked in, would you, and have to spend the night?"

"Oh, could I?" I said. "Please."

She sized me up. "You poor man," she said. "No place to stay?"

It was an understandable mistake — the long black hair, the beard, the heavy boots, worn jeans, flannel shirt, the lanky haggard look, and the mental institute just across the river. "Well . . . " I said.

"I could call a cab. They could take you to a shelter."

"That's not necessary, but tell me this. Who designed this exhibit?" Now that the mood had been shattered, technical questions of hydrology, oxygenation, and finance replaced my longing. I tapped on the glass. "Whose work is this?" The lady looked puzzled. "I'm still trying to make something of my life," I said with absolute honesty. "I haven't given up yet."

"Good for you." She jotted some information on a chit of paper. "Call this number in the morning. Ask for Mr. Eliot. Tell him Bernice Bilodeau said to call."

"Thank you," I said. "Thank you very much."

She reached into her wallet.

I said, "No, really, you don't. . . . "

"Don't be silly," she said, stuffing a twenty dollar bill into my shirt pocket.

"God bless you," I said. "You won't regret this. I promise you."

Outside, the snow looked like the stuff of angels, and, though I wouldn't have wanted to know the pH, it tasted sweet as powdered sugar. This was indeed a charmed moment: my first backer, my very first investor. I made a mental note, a lifetime pass for Bernice Bilodeau to The River Dwight, and on my way home, to honor the occasion, I bought a six-pack of Molson and a bouquet of flowers.

There was a time when Marie would have been touched by the gesture. On the occasions when I forgot that those days were over, she was quick to remind me.

"I don't even want to know where you got the money," she said.

"Like I always say, 'follow your heart and the money will find you.'"

"God, Dwight, you're not twenty years old any more, or even thirty, or even thirty-five, for that matter."

"If you don't like the flowers, have a beer. Have two beers. They might improve your disposition."

I popped my second Molson, warmed myself by the woodstove and thought how really well preserved and fetching Marie looked in her uniform, how pleasingly the pure white offset her black hair and pale blue eyes, how the cut of the dress suited her narrow waist and wide hips. I was feeling pretty good. "Yep," I said, "you had better mark this day down in your little book, because on this day, your husband has had a grand idea."

"My little book is full of your grand ideas. There's not room for any more."

"No, no, your book is full of bright, little ideas, brainstorms, but this, my dear, is different. I have expanded my vision."

"Well, don't. OK?"

"Too late. You can't put the genie back in the bottle."

"God help us." She tossed the flowers into the stove and opened a beer. "I have prayed this day would never come," she said. "I mean, literally prayed, and regularly ever since you spent that whole year working on that dumb mayfly pattern. Day after day, night after night, tying and re-tying, filling the sink and tub with trash, not sleeping, walking the roads day and night for dead animals, stinking up the house with skins — I said the same prayer every night. I said, 'God, please don't let anything run him over, and keep his thinking small,' because I could see then, if you ever came up with a big idea, it would kill you, kill us both."

I had never heard any of that before. "That hurts," I said. "That really hurts. That you don't have any more faith in me than that. That hurts."

"I'm sorry, Dwight. I'm truly sorry, but I'm not going to lie to you."

"Bernice Bilodeau has faith in me. She believes in me, but my own wife . . . "

"I suppose that's the poor soul you fleeced for beer money."

"You know what you are? You're a traitor."

"I am. I know it. My faith in you should be inexhaustible, but it isn't, and now you know. And now I'm going to bed. I've been on my feet all day, and I'm very tired, and I'm going to bed."

"One day you won't have to be on your feet all day."

"No, I'll be in a wheelchair."

For the record Dwight's Perfect Mayfly was featured in *FLYTYER'S NEWS*, Vol. VII, Issue #3, complete with color plates and tying instructions. True, the commercial prospects haven't panned out — so far — but who is to say that even as we sit here the fly's reputation is not spreading by word of mouth, that soon Bean's and Orvis will be forced to carry it in their catalogues, and pay me royalties? Who, really, is to say?

At this point I would like to thank the Taiwanese for having wrested the shoe industry from these labor-beleaguered shores. Not only have they put affordable footwear within easy reach of all Americans, but they also left in their wake a windfall of old, abandoned buildings available to young, or even middle-aged, entrepreneurs at most reasonable prices. I believe this more than compensates for what they have done to us in Little League.

Also I would like to thank Mr. Ronald Reagan for deregulating the Savings & Loan industry, thereby liberating thousands of loan officers from the tedium of home mortgages. All over America, even in Maine, loan officers were ready to celebrate their freedom, and what better place to start than with a local project that would simultaneously revitalize downtown Augusta, give people a warm place to congregate on cold winter nights, keep teenagers off the streets, reduce adolescent pregnancy, curtail the use of drugs, cut crime? "And I wouldn't be surprised if this project slowed the spread of AIDS," I said to the loan officer, one Theresa Bilodeau, no relation to Bernice but a handsome woman in her own right, a rugged business-like blonde who wore her hair in a tidy bun.

She was wearing a conservative grey suit, but so was I. Plus I had shaved my beard and trimmed my hair, shined my shoes and borrowed a brief case. I had also rehearsed my presentation in front of the mirror, there having been no interested parties available. And it was a doozy, if I do say so myself. I could tell Theresa was impressed as she flipped through the computer printouts, plans and blueprints.

"This is all very interesting," she said. I thanked her. "And this project may do everything you say it will, but keep in mind, Kennebec Savings is not a charitable organization. And the first question we have to ask ourselves is, is this project financially viable? Because if the answer to that question is no, then it's not going to do any of these other things, is it?"

"Of course not, but I think you'll find the answer to that question on page four." I had made some earnings projections based on the number of fishermen we could accommodate, charges per hour, food sales, entry fee and so on. "You'll have to admit, those are pretty impressive numbers."

"Indeed they are," she said, after looking them over, "And there are some pretty bold assumptions underlying them. Such as, that you will be operating at full capacity."

"Cut those figures by twenty per cent and we still make a profit."

"Assuming your expenses are in line, which brings up another point. Your previous business experience, or lack thereof. We do like to see previous experience."

"Why? So you can weed out originality, so you can keep repeating yourself?"

"No. Actually it's so that we can remain solvent."

"Theresa, tell me this, how much business experience did Colonel Sanders have?"

"I haven't the faintest idea."

"Not a lick, but he made great chicken and the business took care of itself."

"Is this going to be a franchise?"

"Might be. You don't know. You might be looking at the Colonel Sanders of indoor fishing." I stopped and looked her right in the eye. "Theresa, don't let this rinky-dink town cramp your vision. Don't let it make you afraid to think big. I have seen it happen."

"Didn't happen to you, did it?"

"No, and I don't intend to let it."

She closed the folder. "Well, this is all quite fascinating, to say the least, but the first thing I have to do is run these building estimates by my consultants. Then I'll need to confer with the powers that be. This will take some time. Not too long. Ten to fourteen days. I'll be in touch." She stood up to shake my hand.

"Fourteen days?" I said.

"Is that a problem for you?"

"No, no problem whatsoever. Nice talking to you."

Fourteen days of hell, of suspended animation. I didn't dare leave the house, or clean it, or change clothes. I held myself in a state of readiness. This was the turning point of my life. My past and future would pivot on this moment, I was sure. And I believe I can be forgiven for a momentary lapse of judgment, when, on day fifteen at 0900, the loan came through and I wrapped the check in Marie's dinner napkin. When she found it, she wept and hers weren't tears of joy either.

Probably I don't need to say this, but it's not easy living with a non-fisherman. Non-fishermen tend to view fishing and everything connected with it as a form of goofing off. I have dedicated my life to disabusing people of this notion. Judged by this criterion, my life to that point had not been a resounding success. Possibly I took out my frustration on my workmen.

I drove them hard. I exhorted them with a bullhorn. I put a stopwatch on their lunch hours. I also helped pour concrete, move boulders, and plant shrubs. After ten weeks of work, I felt as if I was earning their respect, but, of course, it wasn't theirs I was after.

I kept Marie away from the project until we had at least a rudimentary river, though not yet one that would support life. That would require gravel, oxygen, and an even temperature, but as soon as we had running water, I took her for a visit. I wanted her to see the river, hear it, feel it, and believe in it, and in me.

I made her keep her eyes closed until we were on the balcony, standing there like the king and queen of England looking down upon our loyal subjects, who, fortunately, were far enough away that we couldn't see their facial expressions. The men all stopped work and looked up at us. They had my permission, my blessing, to take a break at this time — with pay. There were a couple of wolf whistles directed at Marie.

"They like you," I said. She glared at me. "They're looking up my dress." She took a step back. I made a sort of regal gesture with my right hand and a couple of the men made obscene ones in return. "Look over there," I said diverting Marie's attention. "See that stretch of river. We're going to put spawning gravel in there. One day fish will be reproducing in this river, my river, our river."

"I don't see any river," Marie said. "All I see is a lot of dirt and concrete."

"Of course," I said. The river bed was dry. "So. Behold." I gave the thumbs up to one of the men. He flipped a lever, and a great gush of water came pouring forth, flooding the serpentine river bed, creating riffles, pools, deep mysterious runs.

"Ok," Marie said. "I've seen it. Can I go now?"

"That's it? That's all you have to say?"

"Dwight," She said, looking at her feet, "Dear sweet Dwight, I never for one moment doubted you were capable of creating such a thing as this. Only that you could sustain it. Twenty years ago, I found your flashes of brilliance and moments of glory charming. But don't you see, flashes and moments just don't cut it any more. Consistency, stability, that's what I find sexy now." She looked me in the eyes, such sadness. "I'm sorry," she said. "I guess I got old on you. Or middle aged. Please forgive me." She kissed me on the cheek and left. There were tears running down the side of my face, but they were her tears.

The workmen were still looking up at me; they were unnaturally quiet. I lifted my bullhorn. "She likes it," I said, "but she was disappointed that you aren't farther along. Now back to work."

Marie elected not to attend our grand opening. It was probably just as well. It didn't turn out quite the way I planned. People had apparently misunderstood our advertisements. They thought the place was a theme park; they saw the river as a giant waterslide. Some showed up with inner tubes. Others wanted to rent towels. I had to make an announcement over the PA system.

"This is not a carnival ride," I said. "It's a place to fish. there'll be no swimming, no tubing, no canoeing in this river."

This led to an ugly scene, children crying, women shouting. When that group cleared out, that left a mere handful of fishermen, and they wanted to buy worms. "We don't sell worms," I said. "It's flyfishing only, catch and release."

And where were all the flyfishermen? Presumably off fishing real rivers. I'd made a slight miscalculation and opened in June, the peak of fishing season.

Meanwhile the river itself performed magnificently. It produced a steady hatch of mayflies throughout the morning — the only indoor mayfly hatch in America, perhaps the world. Fish were rising over the river's entire sinuous course. By folding it like ribbon candy, I had fit nearly two hundred yards of river into my building. The different stretches were separated by low hills and a blend of real and artificial foliage. Trails linked the better pools. Beside the prime waters, I'd placed picnic tables. But I had left several good sections unmarked and with poorly maintained trails. These would be the rewards of adventurous fishermen, just like in real life.

A family of swallows had found my place, and now nested in the rafters. Opening day they swooped and dove above the river, feeding on the hatching mayflies. "I'm glad you appreciate this place," I said. "I wish more people did."

In August when Maine rivers overheat, trout head for spring holes where they hang out until fall. Fish-hogs find these spring holes and slaughter untold numbers of trout. Ethical fishermen seek alternatives: largemouth bass, yard work, quality time with the family. Now there was a new alternative in town, and right on schedule, predictable as a mayfly hatch, fly fishermen arrived at The River Dwight, the entire local chapter of Trout Fishers United.

Unfortunately, they didn't come to fish. They came to protest the black fly experiments that were being performed in my river.

If I neglected to mention these experiments, it was out of modesty, not shame, for I was proud to have biologists on my premises. I saw their presence as another example of The River Dwight serving the community. Also these biologists were my sole source of mayfly larvae. They provided me mayflies; I let them use my river. They welcomed my offer, because Bti, the substance they were testing, had been banned from natural waterways, no matter that the same substance was widely used in many other states. For political reasons it had been banned by backward Maine. One day the political reasons came calling on The River Dwight.

I was working on a deep bend in the river, rearranging debris that I hoped would conceal fish. Mayflies were popping up all over. I had heard the group was coming, though I didn't know why; so I set the water temperature at sixty-five degrees, ideal for mayflies.

"If you want our patronage," the chapter president said, "these illegal, immoral experiments will have to stop."

I stood up and looked him over. He was medium height and lean, with a narrow face. He wore wire-rimmed glasses, a grey suit and tassel loafers.

"Do you realize that this 'illegal, immoral' substance is used routinely in many other states?"

"That doesn't make it right, or mean it's safe."

"Are you a biologist?"

"No. I'm a lawyer."

"A lawyer! And you presume to instruct me in morality!"

"Right, the old kick the lawyer routine. Let me just tell you one thing. If this situation isn't corrected, not only will you not get our business, but we'll be going public with our information. We worked damned hard to get Bti off Maine rivers, and we will not have our work undone by you."

"Well, I worked damned hard to get Bti *in* my river. I believe in the scientific method, and in free scientific inquiry. And I assure you, The River Dwight will not be blackmailed by frustrated politicians posing as fishermen."

As the group turned to leave, there was a heavy splash behind them where a large trout cleared the water for an escaping dun. A dozen heads spun back towards the water, necks craned. Several members exchanged furtive glances. Then they left, but I knew that they would be back. No real fisherman lets politics stand between him and a mayfly hatch for long. I just wasn't sure my place of business would be there when they did return.

This was an unexpected setback and a difficult one to explain to my creditors. So I decided that for the time being my only recourse was to ignore them. Easier said than done. An insistent group, these creditors, and generally most unsympathetic to the entrepreneurial spirit. Never mind that this spirit is what made America great. Once they got their slice of the pie, all they wanted was to get paid. I found them, on the whole, to be rather rude. They sent threatening notices through the US Mail. They left discourteous messages on my answering machine. Even Theresa Bilodeau, in whom I placed utmost faith, was getting feisty.

Then Marie moved out. Quite in keeping with her personality, there were no theatrics to her departure, no melodrama whatsoever, only the quiet orderly collection of her possessions and the latching of suitcases. I had never realized before how well a suitcase latch could mimic the hammer of a gun. Really quite a startling imitation.

Marie paused at the door. "I don't want to fight about money," she said. "I just want what's rightfully mine."

I said, "Fair enough. According to my figures, you now owe Kennebec Savings eight hundred and fifty thousand dollars."

"Cute."

I walked over to the door. "I'll turn this thing around yet, you'll see. One day we'll look back on this little episode and laugh. This is going to be good for me, Marie. It's going to inspire me to work harder and be more creative. This could be just the incentive I need. Thank you for having the wisdom to do what needed to be done."

"Don't mention it. Would you mind watering the plants until I get situated."

"That's the least I can do."

Different people handle stress in different ways. Some drink, some smoke, some take drugs. I fish. After Marie moved out, I set up housekeeping beside The River Dwight. I moved into a little pup tent beside a beautiful run of water I had dubbed Marie's Run and hadn't got around to renaming. It was an exact replica of the museum pool, enlarged several times.

I've heard it said, "No man is an island." Well, a man is not a river either, but he's more like a river than like an island. And he can learn more from a river. For instance, even oceans contain rivers. There's a lesson in that: rivers don't just drain the land. Rivers are more than water responding to the call of gravity. They're living entities. They link continents; they connect us all, if we let them. And when we forget those connections or deny them or try to sever them, the fish are there to remind us.

One night I caught a twenty-inch brown. No big deal? Consider this: I didn't stock the place with browns. I stocked it with brook trout because they're easy to catch. Browns are too finicky. And this one was no exception.

He was rising steadily at the head of the deepest pool on the river, but he wouldn't take a dry fly. My first reaction was that one of my fish was getting selective. "Don't tell me that," I said. Selectivity really would spell the end of my business. Then I realized the fish wasn't taking duns at all; he was nymphing. I breathed a sigh of relief and tied on a Gold Ribbed Hare's Ear. He took it on the first pass. When I struck, he jumped and that was when I realized it wasn't a brook trout at all; it was a brown and a big one at that. "What the devil?" I said. "Where did he come from?" He had to come from the Kennebec. That was where I got my water; it was where my effluent went, but there were screens, pumps and filters. A unit must have failed, but I would worry about that later.

He fought hard enough, but I had on a 2X tippet. I tightened the drag and stifled his runs. I wanted this fish, and soon I had him. I dragged him up onto a patch of gravel and grabbed him with both hands. He was so fat I could barely get my hands around him. As he lay there gasping for air, his mustard yellow sides speckled brightly in red and black, the businessman in me said, "Kill him." Browns this size are cannibals; he would eat his weight in brook trout every week. I took out my pocket knife, and prepared to rap him over the head, but the fisherman in me stayed my hand. I could buy more brook trout, but I couldn't replace a fish like this. Truth was, I was honored by this fish's presence in my river, however it was he gained entry.

I waded into the shallows and held the fish in the current. I held him longer than was necessary. I didn't want to kill him, but I didn't want to let him go either. I just wanted to stand there in the river holding him. Finally the fish lost patience and freed himself.

Meanwhile Theresa Bilodeau was having a relationship with my answering machine. They were not getting along. No matter now conciliatory she sounded, ("We want to work with you, Dwight"), no matter how subtly threatening ("We're bankers, not realtors"), or not so subtly ("Don't force our hand"), she got the same recorded message.

The only message that I answered during those troubled times was Marie's: "Where are my plants?" she asked. "I want them back. You had no right to make off with my plants."

I left a message on her answering machine. I said, "The plants have found a new home. They are very happy here, but they do miss their mother. Please feel free to visit. We are open seven days from six to ten, three dollars an hour for adults, twelve and under a dollar fifty. Thank you for calling The River Dwight."

Name, rank and serial number, that was my philosophy. If they wanted more, they knew where to find me.

Funny how much genuine peace and solitude a man can find beside an artificial river. In some ways it was better then the real thing, because there were no chain saws buzzing in the background, no drunks on ATV's, no radios. Just the sound of the river at whatever flow rate I wanted, in whatever season. If only I could have shut out the other world forever.

But I couldn't. There were bills, letters, nasty messages. Soon, I had the same beleaguered feeling I sometimes had in the real Maine woods, when I'd sense the outside world slowly closing in, the spray planes and logging rucks, and chainsaws. Gradually I came to realize that I couldn't escape the so-called "civilized" world. Whether in the form of financial pressures or treachery of the paper industry, one way or the other, civilization was going to have its way with what was left of wilderness. The best I could hope for was that in the wake of the chainsaws and ATV's some new form of wildness would arise, like grass sprouting in sidewalk cracks, or, for that matter, wild brown trout breaking and entering a man-made river.

Be all that as it may, there's still only so much crap you are required to take, and I was getting sick and tired of the steady stream of letters the TFU folks were sending to the *Kennebec Journal*. So, I fired off a little salvo of my own in the form of a full page ad:

*While The River Dwight wholeheartedly supports Trout Fishers United, and its goals of protecting and enriching cold water fisheries, we sincerely regret that this support is not reciprocal. We further regret that TFU allows itself to be represented in the press by a small-minded, mean-spirited, loud-mouthed minority of its members. We abhor its unfair characterization of our facility and of the legitimate scientific research being conducted on our premises.*

*We would like to reassure our loyal patrons that The River Dwight is in no way "polluted" and that Bacillus thuringiensis israelensis (Bti) is a totally inocuous organism, and perfectly harmless to humans. We would remind our patrons that yogurt is made from bacteria and wine from yeast, though this is in no way intended to imply that Bti is fit for human consumption or is of nutritional or medicinal value.*

*Finally, we would like to assure our faithful creditors that this is a minor, temporary setback that will in no way affect our long range profitability. Third quarter projections remain robust as ever. These things happen; then they pass, but The River Dwight will abide forever.*

The very next evening on my way up the street to buy a paper to see how the TFU boys handled that, who should I run into but Theresa Bilodeau.

"Theresa," I said, "what a surprise. Long time no see. How've you been?" I tried to get around her, but she reached out and grabbed my arm. "You can't run away from this, Dwight," she said. "This is not the type of relationship you can simply turn your back on when the going gets tough."

"Damn it," I said. "You've been talking to Marie."

"She came to us. She was concerned. She still cares, though I'm not sure exactly why."

"She cares about her plants."

"She cares about a lot more than that. Now stop acting like a child, come inside. We're going to talk."

I looked at my watch.

"Not later, not tomorrow. Now!"

"OK, OK, great. I want to talk to you. We have a lot to talk about. But look, give me five minutes to fix the place up. It's a mess. Five minutes, is that too much to ask?"

"Is there another exit?"

"Theresa!"

"Five minutes," she said. "The meter's running."

One thing I was particularly proud of, in addition to my mayflies, was the computerized rheostats that controlled lights, sound, air and water temperatures, wind conditions, and humidity. With a control panel no more complex than a VCR's I could program background music, birdsongs, wind and with the magic of track lighting, the exact solar arc of every season — except winter. There was no winter on The River Dwight.

With enough time I believe I could have come up with a more suitable program for Theresa. If only I had known her better, her tastes in music, her moods, her emotional needs. But I didn't have more time, so I went with my old standbys: Wynette's "Stand By Your Man." It was one of Marie's favorites, mine too. It was our song. With Theresa it was a shot in the dark, but what did I have to lose?

I ushered Theresa inside into total blackness. "I can't see a thing," she said. "It's cold too." She shivered.

I put an arm around her. "It's pre-dawn," I whispered. "Imagine we have just driven two hours to the trail head. Listen to the river. And look, to the east." There was a faint orange glow on the far wall. A bird chirped, and a soft warming breeze whooshed through the foliage. More birds. The orange intensified; the center filled with red, and the chorus of "Stand By Your Man" synchronized itself to dawn. When there was sufficient light, I took Theresa's arm and escorted her down the narrow trail towards the river. We stood at the water's edge and watched morning emerge in all its artificial

glory. A trout rose in mid-stream.

"Did you see that?"

She nodded.

Then the music died and the moment passed and it was morning like any other summer morning. "So," I said, "what do you think of The River Dwight now?"

She shook her head in what I took to be amazement. "I think I know why you've been late with your payments."

"You didn't like it."

"That's not what I said."

"It was the music, wasn't it? It was a cliche. If only I'd had more time to prepare. I can do Billy Joel, Thelonious Monk, James Taylor. You name it."

"I believe you. Completely. I think that's part of the problem."

"What? It's overdone?"

She looked at me and smiled and nodded. It was a sweet, sad, eerily familiar smile. "You shouldn't have come to a bank for a loan. You should have applied to the Maine Arts Commission."

It was Marie's smile, and I was about to hear what a clever fellow I was, and I was sick of it, even if I had brought it on myself. "I'm not an artist," I said. "I'm a businessman."

"You could have fooled me."

"I fooled a lot of people. But the fact is, I never had an original idea in my life. Everything I've ever done has been begged, borrowed or stolen. Including the idea for this river."

It felt good to admit that. I felt like a weight had been lifted from my shoulders, and a veil from my eyes, and for the first time I could see clearly what had to happen next. The river told me: trout were making redds; they were about to spawn in this very run, and those trout and this river had to be protected at all cost. I didn't have the right to let them be destroyed. The fact was, the dream had outgrown the dreamer, and the purity of my original vision seemed trivial compared to the living reality of the river.

I turned back to Theresa. She was still eyeing me with sympathy and concern. "Theresa, I said I was a businessman. I didn't say I was a good businessman."

She nodded and seemed relieved by my confession, as if

now my rehabilitation could begin.

"It's possible," I said, "that I might have overestimated the amount of income fishermen were going to generate."

"That sounds plausible."

"By the same token, though, I may have underestimated other potential sources of revenues, that I'm just now beginning to explore. The truth is, Theresa, I have expanded my vision of The River Dwight. Walk over here with me, would you?"

We cut through a wooded section to my campsite. There was the tent and my Coleman stove and my flyrod propped against a tree. "Here's a little concept I've been working on," I said. "Campsites beside the river. Theresa, think of all the people who get camping gear for Christmas and then have to wait five or six months to use it. How many of those people do you think would like a chance to try out that new sleeping bag or that new tent in the winter? Beside a river, a river with real live fish in it?"

"Interesting concept."

"I could easily expand my fishing shop to handle camping gear. It would be a natural tie-in. I've pretty much decided to add a few other stores, maybe on a second floor, not to obstruct the sky light, but, you know ... "

"A mezzanine?"

"Exactly! You read my mind. And maybe a little boutique." Marie always wanted a boutique.

"Sort of a mall concept."

I winced. "Well, I wouldn't call it that," I said. "but you can if you like. But it couldn't interfere with the river. That's one rule. Everything revolves around the river."

"Of course, it does. It wouldn't work any other way."

"You understand, Theresa, these renovations are going to require some additional funds. Probably we should talk about restructuring the loan."

"Probably we should," she said.

I could see that word meant a lot to her. "Re-structuring." It sounded responsible and business-like. So I used it several more times, and I kept talking like that until the last vestiges of pity were gone from her eyes.

# Going Fishing

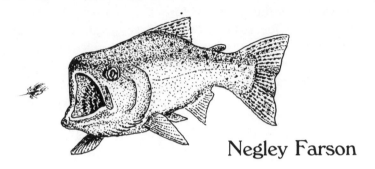

Negley Farson

There was one year when I fished four countries: Chile, England, France, and Norway. This was in 1937, at the end of which the Norwegians asked me to write the fishing chapter in their Sports Club yearbook. It was a pleasant compliment from a race which I greatly admire. And another Scandinavian to whom I loaned the book liked it so much I have not been able to get it back from him since.

Chile is one of the most sporting countries in the world. The Chileans themselves are quite possibly its finest horsemen; they come as close to being Centaurs as modern man and horse can get — at any rate, when you see them riding, either on hacienda or at one of their famous horse shows, both man and horse seem made of one piece, with one brain and with one synchronised system of muscles; and an American cavalry team with which I went down to Valparaiso told me after the competition that they had never seen such horsemen in their life. This was from men of the famous USA cavalry school at Fort Riley, at least one of whom had jumped at Olympia. There is a legend that when the Spaniards first landed on the coast in their conquest of Peru, the Indians (who had never seen a horse) fled in terror because they thought both horse and man were one — were monsters — until one Conquistador was knocked off his horse . . . and the Indians attacked.

But it was an Irishman who introduced fishing into Chile — its magnificent Rainbow trout. I saw quite a lot of him in Valparaiso; a big, genial grey-haired man who had been honorary game warden for the country (self-appointed, I believe), patron of both the horse racing and the famous shows; who, twenty-five years before, had hit on the idea of introducing some Rainbow trout into the swift, green, rapid-streaked rivers that flow down from the Southern Andes. The result has been a miracle. These streams are simply crawling with crayfish — and a Rainbow likes nothing better; until within even the last few years some of them were never fished; and the Rainbow (with that predilection of theirs for travel) have spread all over the country. They might not reach the size of those prodigious Rainbow of New Zealand, but if for fitness and fighting quality they may have their equals, I doubt if finer Rainbow can be found anywhere else in the world.

The result of this is that in Valparaiso and Santiago you find colonies of Irish, English, Scots, and American — men from the old nitrate days or the modern copper mines — who, almost the minute they have met you, take you to their homes and show you their rods and tackle, produce a whisky bottle, and in a few minutes are telling you fish stories that make even you blush to listen.

The funny part of it is, they are true. One naval attaché said to me, "When I wrote home and told my friends that the first four Rainbows I caught in Chile averaged over six pounds, they wrote back and called me a liar!" I merely nodded my head — for, only a few days previously at a strange shoot arranged for the Diplomatic Corps on the hitherto preserved lakes supplying the water to Valparaiso, I had seen this same man kill forty-eight ducks in one morning, shooting through a hole in a blind (which I had in the afternoon) with only a 20-bore shotgun. It was even said that his country had appointed him to Chile in particular simply because its State Department knew his passion and skill with both rod and gun would make him a success with the sporting Chileans.

He was one.

There is a Scot in Valparaiso, the third generation of his family to be born in the country, who is reputed to be the best

fly fisherman in Chile. He came into my room in the hospital
where I was lying, introduced himself, and said, "When you get
out of here I am going to give you some fishing that will take
the hair off your head." The naval attaché whom I have just
mentioned assured me that this was only the bare truth. And
the ambassador of my own country (a fanatic fisherman
himself) gave me four of the best and biggest Silver Doctors in
his book. "You will need plenty of backing on the river where
that man is going to take you!" he warned me. When I told him
the size of my two reels and the weight of the rod he closed his
eyes and said: "Well, then, there's no use going. They'll just run
away from you . . . take the lot!"

It didn't sound promising. But I was used to this rod and
thought it was better to stick to the devil I knew rather than
accept one of the longer and more powerful rods which the
Scot tried to lend me. Also, going off with such a reputedly fine
fisherman I did not want to take the chance of performing with
a rod that might make me look clumsy. So a few nights later he
and I and an English ex-naval officer (who had been in the
Secret Service in Chile during the last war) were in a train for
southern Chile — for Chillan, the town which was literally
wiped off the map by an earthquake a few years later. From
Chillan we drove the next day, some forty or fifty miles, I think,
to a little village between us and the far, blue, broken silhouette
of the Andes. After that there was nothing between us and the
mountains but a grim plain of low scrub, roadless and rocky.
When the next morning we forced the unfortunate car we had
procured through this sea of low undergrowth we passed an
occasional horseman who, in this setting, brought back pictures
of remote Spain. For he sat his horse with the same idle
arrogance; he wore a flat black hat, such as you will see in
Andalusia; he was Spanish (with possibly a dash of Indian
blood); and about the only essential outward difference was
that *this* man held his hat to his head by a strap that was tied to
his nose! There is a little black tippet dangling from it that
always makes you think these Chilean caballeros' noses must
be bleeding. The one or two horsemen we met merely gave us a
solemn nod, by way of salute; but an old hag that we came on,
a withered old ancient riding side-saddle, cackled at us when

she watched us get out of the car and put our slender rods together by the banks of the racing river. The blue Andes never seemed to have come any nearer; they lay always like a jagged line of broken blue glass along the eastern sky.

What made it even more strange was that the volcano of Chillan, on our left, was erupting every ten minutes. So regularly that you could set your watch by it, it shot 2,000-foot feather of sulphur yellow into the blue sky every ten minutes. And three times when I had on my first fish I saw that feather shoot up.

This river was the Laja, racing down from the extinct volcano of Antuco in the far Andes. In the long flat sweeps it was a deep bottle-green . . . but swirling. Then it crashed through the rocks it had rounded through the ages, poured white over ledges, and emitted the continuous low roar of broken water. I remembered what the ambassador had told me in Santiago — "plenty of backing on your line" — and my heart sank.

At any rate, I told myself, put on the biggest leader you've got (it was a 2X), soak it well . . . and trust to heaven. It was well I did.

I had picked the side of a broad stretch of white falls where the main river swept past in frothing white water and where there was a lee of green water lying along the main current. I felt that if there were any big trout, waiting for something to come down, this was where they would be. It was easy casting, for there was no high brush behind me, and I kept as long a line as I could in the air, hoping to reach the edge of the white water. I think I must have been even more shocked than the fish when, on my very first cast, just as my fly was sweeping down about opposite me, I got that driving pull of a heavy strike. It was the first cast I made in Chile — and it was the best fish.

Without waiting for any more argument he went straight on down the river, sweeping through the white water, where he seemed to rest, or sulk, for a moment in the green water on the other side. It was lucky for me that he did; practically every foot of my line had been taken out. So there we were. I could not get across to him. Neither could I get him across to me. So I gave him the bend of the rod while I stood there and thought about it.

In these parts of Chile there is a very poor brand of peasant, which exists heaven knows how; they come about as close to living without any visible means of support as you would think man could get. There was the brush-board-and-thatched hovel of one of these ramshackle humans behind me now. Its inhabitants had evidently been watching me for some time. Now, seeing me standing there, apparently doing nothing, a small urchin impelled by curiosity came cautiously up to see what I was doing. We spoke no language in which we could communicate with each other; and when I unhooked my landing-net and snapped it open he almost fainted from fright. But he was a quick-witted little fellow, and, somehow, he comprehended what a net was. I made him take it from me.

So there were two of us standing there now. The fish had remained exactly where he was. I gave him a slow pull. The next instant the fish was going down along his side of the river and the boy and I were stumbling down along the boulders on ours. As I said, these strange, volcanic rocks had been rounded by time, and a more tricky, stumbling, infuriating river journey I have seldom made. For I was deep in the river by now, getting as close to the fish as I could get in order to win back some more line. In this fashion I took several yards back from him. Then I reached a high stretch of bank where the water was too deep, and so came back to land. It was now, I said gloomily to myself, that I would lose this fish. I remembered the big sea trout I had had on for two hours and forty minutes in the Shetlands. Here was to be another broken heart; for, some fifty yards below me, shone a long sloping shelf of white water in the mid-day sun.

Then the fish took it into his head to command operations. To my confused delight and dismay he came directly at me across the white water, so fast that I could barely strip in the line. I had no chance to reel in. Then he went on up the river, taking the line with him as fast as I could pay it out without fouling it. Then, boring against the line, as if he meant to jump the low falls, he again remained stationary over one spot.

This was exactly what the doctor ordered. I could not have asked him to do anything nicer. Reeling in as swiftly as I could, I worked my way up to him. So there, plus one Chilean boy, we were exactly where we had started over twenty minutes before. I knew it was twenty minutes, because twice during our tussle, I had seen Chillan erupt. That 2,000-foot sulphurous jet!

Now began one of the most beautiful battles I have ever experienced. For I had plenty of line in hand now; when he came past I gave him the bend of the rod for all I thought it could stand — determined he should never cross to the other side of that white water again. And every time I checked him. The green water was so glass-clear that when he swung in the swirls sluicing past me the sun caught and reflected the pinkish stripe along his strong sides. I could watch him fighting the hook. And then he spun in the sun, jumping. He was the very essence of fight. Furious, I think — still not frightened.

There is no doubt that in the ingredients of a fisherman's delight there is nothing comparable to being able to watch a fish fight like this. For I could see him, or his shape, nearly all the time. Chillan erupted once more.

But by now my gallant Rainbow was a slow-moving, sullen thing. His tail worked heavily, he lay in the green water about twenty yards out from me. And I looked around for the lee of some rocks and slowly worked him in. I had him in a pool. It was almost still water. He was almost resting against the hook. And then, as the bank was high, and I was an idiot, I signalled the little Chilean boy to wade out and slip the net under him . . .

The boy did. He was an eager boy . . . so eager that he stabbed the net at the fish . . . pushed him with it! Then he tried to scoop him in from the tail . . . I jumped. As I did, the boy actually got the fish into the net. I seized boy, net, fish, all at the same time, and threw them all up on the bank. There I dived on the fish.

It all goes to prove the hysterical condition into which some fishermen will get themselves. For this Rainbow was not much over six pounds. But he was such a beautiful one! That was the point; that small nose, and those deep shoulders, and those firm fighting flanks. This fish had been living in clean water on crayfish galore. I sat on the bank and looked at him for nearly twenty minutes. I had him.

Then I sighed, got up, and went to fishing again.

I got three more fish that afternoon. The next one was a five-and-a-half-pounder. He put up a grand fight. But it was not the same thrill. I felt braver now; I could afford to be more rough with them. I could take time out to watch . . . this great river sweeping down in the sun below me. I noticed that on nearly all the flat rocks were the crushed shells of crayfish. Eaten there by some form of bird, obviously. And then, as I was fishing one point, a flock of reddish duck came round it so swiftly they almost swept into me. The Scot, that beautiful fly-caster (and he certainly was one!) had taken one look at my six-pounder, and immediately set off down river — determined to catch a bigger one. The English ex-naval officer had also examined it. "Ah," was all he said. Then he went up the river and began fishing furiously below another fall.

Meantime, I caught two more three-pounders.

I suddenly became aware that I was very fatigued (for I have one leg which is not quite so good as the other), and I hooked the faithful fly into the cork handle of my rod, tipped the little Chilean brat, and worked back to the car. There I found the Scot and the Englishman, who held the bottle out to me . . .

"Funny, isn't it," smiled the Englishman as I wiped my lips, "how damned *good* it tastes after a day like this! Nothing like the same taste in the city . . . "

"Ah . . . ," I said — and looked eagerly at their catch.

They were all spread out on the grey boulders. We each had four fish. And I had the biggest. "It's been a grand day!" I said comfortably.

That ride home, when you're tired — that's another one of the delights of a day's fishing. We could rest in the car. The whisky gave a certain romanticism to our conversation. "And they feed you well at this pub," said the Scot. "We've taught these people how to cook — we'll probably have some duck tonight."

"But what about the *Rainbows?*" I gasped.

They smiled at me pityingly. The Rainbows, their smiles indicated, would be cooked for me in due course, and in the correct manner. In the meantime we drove through the little Spanish-like village as night came down, dragged off our heavy waders, had a good sponge bath in a clay room off the patio, and got into fresh, light clothes. On our way out to where the buckets of cool water awaited us we passed through the kitchen — and there I saw two fat Spanish-looking women splitting our trout, and hanging them on hooks (like shirts to be dried!) above the clay stove. My big one was being cut into sections for immediate boiling.

The next morning we had him — with a bottle of that splendid Chilean Hock — cold for breakfast. It was the sybaritish send-off for another day of the most splendid fishing.

But on this day I disgraced myself. I not only caught another five-and-a-half-pounder, but I also caught the most fish. I led by one. And this one, I was made to feel, should never have been taken. The Scot looked grim.

"What!" I cried. "You mean to tell me that you throw back two-and-a-half-pounders?"

They merely nodded. The implication was that in order to beat them I had taken a fish undersize. I then told them that truly they had taken the hair off my head — as I would off any fisherman to whom I tried to tell this story.

I must admit that a bottle of good white wine for breakfast is not quite the accepted way to start off a day's fishing. Yet there is the stirrup cup, and the hunting breakfast — not altogether a dry one — and there was a vigorousness in the wild Chilean scene, with the blue thunder of the Andes always in your consciousness, that made such a breakfast just right. My objection to drink (in connection with fishing) is that I know of no other sport where the slightest befuzzlement has such disastrous results. I don't mean merely that you will almost certainly hook yourself, but as the whole art of fly-casting consists in knowing — in your subconscious mind — exactly where the fly is, even when it is behind you, you need a head clear as crystal to know what you are about. I know. I have fished after too good a lunch at a river inn, and had the whole afternoon spoiled for me. I didn't enjoy it. The loveliness of running water was dulled, the leaves lost their sheen . . . and some stretches of water up which I would have waded with delight on a fresh morning . . . now looked too hard to fish.

That is an unorthodox discussion, but this is an unorthodox book. I must admit my two companions did not like the white wine idea; that was mine. But they had even wilder ideas.

For instance, on our return after the second day's fishing — when I brought in that measly little two-and-a-half-pound

Rainbow — the Scot was told something that plunged him into a desperate mood.

"It's no use," he growled to the Englishman as we were eating our dinner (baked trout this time). "We've got to clear out!"

When I asked what catastrophe had happened to their miraculous strip of river, it turned out that the Scot had just been told that an Indian had reported he had seen another man fishing about ten miles down. Ten miles, mind you.

"Yes, it's too crowded," they agreed in chorus.

"That's the trouble," continued the Scot. "Find a good river . . . go back to Santiago . . . and just *mention* what you've caught on it — and they come down after you like a flock of damn' gulls!"

They had intended to put a shack on this lonely stretch of the Laja: this horse-country of arrogant Chileans with their hats held on by nose straps. To me it seemed about as barren and barbaric a bit of country as one could wish.

"But now," said the Scot, "we are going to try further up. After you go . . . Jack and I are going to try another river I know of in the Andes."

And so I left them, they going off across the scrub country where Chillan was shooting its yellow jet into the cloudless sky, I to go down to the snow-capped volcanoes of the lake country and cross a pass into Patagonia.

# Deschutes Journal

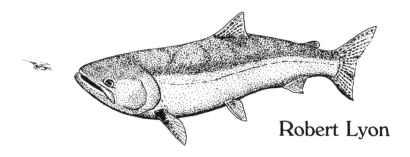

Robert Lyon

It is company policy to put passengers ashore at the head of Whitehorse Rapid. The Deschutes is running true to form today, a collage of broken greens, black and whites. We look for new obstacles: sunken boats, boulders, snags. We check the river height and speed, show the guys our route, answer questions. It always seemed simple enough from the scouting point. Then we hike upstream to our boats, trim them, and push off.

We approach the head of Whitehorse in single file, a hundred feet apart. The Mutton Mountains rise in shadow around us. Clients gather on the bluff along the tracks with cameras. When I see Gordy drop from view ahead of me I catch the oars on the back of my knees, spit on my hands, and stand up. A hundred trips down the Deschutes and still there is a moment of self-checking, of doubt. But at the brink I am dead on. The river quickens. I sit down, level my blades and find my pull-strap with my toes.

The crash of water fills the morning air with a heady blend of nitrogen and thunder. It is intensely exhilarating. I hold my breath and drop at an angle through the big waves at the slot, then wait; one, two, as the boat rocks wildly; then pivot sharply and pull from my anchored foot, and pull some more to be sure. The hull of an aluminum boat like the one I am rowing is wrapped gravely around O Shit rock below, deflecting in the heavy hydraulics like the wing of some strange craft. I put it off my bow and pass within inches.

We run the boulder field below standing up, alone in our driftboats like halfbacks in the secondary, always relieved to be downstream of Whitehorse. The tempo is slower now, the rage cooled. We pull ashore a quarter mile down and await the troops. There is an informal ceremony about having a beer after a safe passage of Whitehorse. I pay my respects. Gordy has pop.

The company menu has not changed since I can remember: steaks the first night out to ease the transition, chicken the next night to get involved with, hamburger the third night when you're too happy and tired to care, and steak again, like cognac, at the end. Greg Kohn, the roustabout, has the second night fruit salad and french bread ready on the table. Gordon Nash, the brilliant moody head guide for the company, has the barbecue chicken close to done.

I go over to Greg with my coffee. He is big, gruff, likeable, a wildlife management graduate from Oregon State. I turn to Greg for more answers out here than I'd care to admit. He is fishing tonight; we are in Lockit.

"All right," Gordy announces. "Dinner's ready." Sitting by the firebox he has his cigarette stuck up out of the corner of his mouth like a chimney. The company has a rep for coming off a little preppy, a little cool sometimes, but there is eccentric genius here; it is a thinking operation, a working blend of intellect and instinct, and the company appeals to a good many fishermen. Gordy has his battered up-and-downer on now; his face is hidden behind the brim, his sunglasses, and his beard. He is inscrutable. The impression comes to me — he is a reflection of his wading mentor, the blue heron. The chicken tongs he wields so deftly are his beak; his long bare legs are a bird's; his enormous wading shoes complete the image. I smile and tell him this. He jabbers his tongs in mock bird at me. Don't we all assume caricature out here.

In the shadow of every tree there is someone. Some are awake and tying leaders or smoking; a few are drinking beer; some are talking. It is the infantry waiting to attack, a rock group waiting to perform. But they are hungry and gather in the kitchen, while I take a minute to sit alone by the water.

We are early walking in the evening sun, Don and I, hiking the old railroad grade to the bend. Greg has rowed across with Mike and Kenny. Gordy's people are spread around the camp water. There is shade everywhere now but the bend. Behind the loading corral a chipped, black enamel cup floats in a cistern. We sip at the cool spring water and pick at the dusty blackberries. The sun is up still, barely an inch of it, emptying through a notch up the west canyon wall. A flurry of jetboat activity heads upstream or down for the evening fish. We watch and wait.

I think how the revolution of the earth regulates our fishing in the canyon (more so than anywhere I know of), how between darkness and direct light we have our moment, quartering flies downstream and swimming them across on a taut, floating line. The Deschutes is a powerful, turbulent river (*River of the Falls*, the French fur traders called it). At no point do you wade across, and only the spoon and plug fishermen easily reach bottom. But the beauty of fishing summer steelhead, anyway, is fishing the lighter tackle, the floating lines, watching the track of your fly across the river surface and the boil of a fish behind. The sun is down suddenly and Don scrambles down the bank.

The Deschutes is an extraordinary deep green color and the visibility is limited, but the big rocks come up nearly to the surface below. I can see the black tops about three feet underwater. Fly fishermen fish the inside of this bend and plug fishermen work the center channel, but the water hugging the outer bank is left alone. I follow Don along the bend tonight, walking quietly above him on the dusty grade.

Fishing an extremely short line over the boulders near shore, I see Don's first fish come up below. The river is so green, though, the first thing I notice is its mouth, the white of its mouth. I start to say something, to tell Don, but as my own mouth opens there is an immense boil where the fly had been and a terrible sudden whine from the reel. A moment later the rod is literally jerked into the river. My mouth is still open watching Don dive in after it.

While Don is wringing out, I replace his twenty pound tippet with ten, dig out the bird's nest and lighten the drag a skosh. I feel bad, as it was my salmon reel I had loaned him when his went down, and I had forgotten to switch it over for steelhead. I remember Marinaro's description of a trout taking in moving water: " ... the swivel of a fish in synchrony with the opening and closing of its jaws as it seizes the fly ... a tail-lashing, lightning-like swivel ... ". Lightning-like describes it pretty well, and from a bright steelhead in heavy water, well ...

During the next hour Don succeeds in raising two more fish among the sunken rocks, but they short-take him each time. I noticed him tense up at each touch now, then at dusk we find ourselves at the end of the bend, walking through the short grass by the water.

It is a curious end to a broad bend in the river here, where the bottom slopes up to a shallow lava plateau, and the river swings back on itself, but not all of the water falls away. The top layer of it sweeps over the lava shelf on our bank and runs for fifty yards before finally joining the main current downstream. It is a hidden tail-out; many fishermen miss it. It is a shoulder of water just above where the river necks, and it is a favorite of mine. The water reminds me of a picture of Grimsa's Strengir Pool, the way lava shelves surround and interlace it. The water is intricate and difficult, but controlled, like a chess game; it requires finesse to wade, to position yourself correctly, and to fish. I show Don the trick to wading it, then sit back against a rock and dig out my pipe. After only a very few minutes Don's fly is pulled under by yet another fish which shoots out to the edge of the pool and holds for a moment while the line catches up, then the fish shakes its head and swims like a bullet into the riffle below. Don hurries ashore and runs out of sight downstream after it.

Walking back in the dark together above the river, Don tells me about this last fish. It was bigger than most, he says, probably twelve to fifteen pounds. It porpoised once on its way to the mouth and never slowed on its second run. He had kept up with it at first, then lost ground gradually for about a quarter-mile before losing it altogether. He is happy though. The air is warm, still, from the heat of the day. Stars sparkle like glitter overhead. Nighthawks flit over the river like bats. We stop at the corral again for drinks and berries, while across the river a Burlington Northern powers laboriously into the interior. It is lovely out and lovely to have gone as far out of camp as we have and now to walk leisurely back in the dark together.

A flashlight signals upstream. I suspect it is Greg with Mike and Kenny from across the river. We wonder how they did. We can see well enough on the road not to bother with a light, but I tap for snakes with my ski pole out of habit, then near camp we turn on our lights and drop off the road and cut through the towering sagebrush toward the river.

Our lawn chairs form a half circle against the water that night. The driftboats are pulled tight against the clay bank and tied off to roots. The 17-foot Havasu is tied up double end and looks as if it will need air again by morning. We are encamped, luckily, in the verdant Park Camp. Precious green grass grows along the water here under the alder trees that grow at regular intervals along the bank. The air is cool and lovely, the river broad and steady flowing. The iced coolers are visited repeatedly. A three-quarter moon has risen and floods the canyon in a flat ivory light.

Everyone is ebullient, smiling. The trip has reached its zenith early, and with luck, will plateau the remaining days. Gordy delivers his gas pump joke. There is laughter, another joke, more laughter; I admire Gordy's abstinence. There are recantations of the day's fish and last year's fish, and talk of fish tomorrow. It is hard to say which is enjoyed most now, the fishing or the collaborating. And doesn't that mark the zenith?

It is late finally. Everyone has straggled off to bed. The sounds of the canyon come alive in the silence; the breeze overhead in the trees, the cough of waves along the clay bank, the hissing lantern. I turn out the light and sit alone by the water a little while longer, but eventually I get up too, making sure camp is adequately windproofed and skunkproofed, remembering to get my journal out of the drywell in the boat, then wander out of camp to bed.

*Deschutes/August 10th/Midnight: Writing this in a growing cloud of caddisflies and aquatic moths and God knows what else. Gordon insists there are species of insects along the Deschutes unknown to modern science. They are a damned nuisance whatever they are, but I should be thankful, I suppose, we have no mosquitoes.*

*Everyone has hooked up already. Kenny O'Rouark is top rod in my boat with four, then Don with two, Mike Leary three; three great fishing friends these guys, their third year back with us. Kenny is co-owner of a fly shop in Reno and fishes throughout the west as much as anyone I know. Mike owns an auto body shop there. Don Kemp is a neurosurgeon out of San Francisco, the straight man of the bunch who fishes the winter-run northern California streams and keeps telling me how much he prefers instead the lighter, floating lines we use here on the Deschutes. Absolutely.*

*Hot today — 105 degrees in the shade on Kohn's thermometer. On the water very early tomorrow: The ledges, Kloan. It's tough to catch up on sleep getting up at three, going to bed at midnight. We're burning our candles at both ends with only two days at home to recoup, then back on the river again. It reminds me of working the hotshot crew — that dazed, dreaming feeling — in Colorado years ago, except the duty is better (to say the least); we may be dazed, sunburned, and hung over, but we are catching great fish on light tackle like nobody's business, eating like kings, and having a fine time in camp to boot. There are worse ways to make a living.*

3:30 am. Up with Greg this morning under a balmy black sky, bumbling around camp in the dark lighting lanterns and stoves, getting breakfast going, coffee going before we roust the troops. There is delicious sliced cantaloup and honeydew on the table, and danish, and a huge pot of black coffee on the Coleman. While the fellows stand around in the kitchen, I take a moment to get into my waders, then go over to Gordy with my coffee and lay plans for the day.

Before long I hear voices out on the water and in the light of the lantern I see Mike standing knee deep in the current holding the boat with one hand, sipping his coffee with the other. Kenny and Don are sitting in the boat.

"Did you get a thermos of coffee?" I call out, hoping they may have forgotten something.

"Hell yes," they laugh. "We're waiting for you."

I smile to myself and pick my vest off a nail in a tree. Sometimes you couldn't pry your guys out of the sack, other times they came to fish. I find my staff and discover they have already loaded my rod. The water is cool against my legs wading out. Mike hauls himself aboard and climbs into his seat. I wag the oars a couple times to get my bearings, then ferry to mid-river where the current sweeps us.

With the coffee the excitement comes into me; we are on the water at the break of day with ten miles of river in front of us, a fine feeling. Gordy will hit camp water and the bend and drop later in the day. We will fish our way downstream and secure a camp in Kloan.

The boat is quiet in the dark; voices are subdued. We pass Harris Canyon. I see a tent pitched there; there is just enough light now reflected off the water. A couple miles further I drop Kenny at Corchy's and tell him to meet us downstream below the old boxcar. We float farther down and put Don ashore, then pulling hard into the current I stand up and peer out over the water for my cue. Just downstream the water runs oily over the ledges. The surface of the river for a hundred square yards has this lovely, oily sheen to it and, again, it reminds me of Iceland.

A canyon opens to the west. In the graying light I see a truck leading a phalanx of dust a mile off, hauling down the west bank. The highest canyon strata now to the east are lit up in lovely pastel colors. There is no wind at all.

I find the bit of sunken shelf where the water nearly breaks running over it and nose into an even pocket of water behind and ship the oars and jump. I take the anchor and wedge it in a smooth lava trough, wetting my bare arm to the shoulder. Then, wading together over the shallow ledges, staring down into the water like blind men with our glasses on and one hand cupped over them to try and distinguish the shelf from the deep green of the troughs that intersect them, we approach the channel near shore. I turn regularly to check on the boat, then show Mike the way to a safe casting station and return hastily, smiling, remembering Jerry Swanson swimming for the raft below the caretaker's ranch my rookie season out. It would not do to lose the boat again today.

When I make it back to the boat, Mike has a long line out sweeping the channel between the ledges and shore. He's in luck and finds a fish right off. We watch it shoot like a bullet over the shallow ledges. He catches it finally and releases it, then hooks two more below the trees in the same channel between the ledges and shore. One of them runs him around the anchor rope. A passing sled has slowed to watch. I take solace in knowing it is hard to get a sled in here, then think how important it is to cultivate your approach on the river: running a driftboat, raft, or sled — each has its advantage. Then I see Don, below us now, fishing the channel along shore and it looks like he is into a fish too; we hear a loud whoop from him. I haven't seen Kenny, though, and I wonder if he has passed us on the grade or is still up at Corchy's.

We get into the boat and drop thirty yards to another ledge and jump out and work it, but turn nothing, then get back in and drop through the big, standing waves at the bottom. If Kenny is not below us around the point I will have to hike up and look for him.

But Kenny, it turns out when we meet up with him around the corner, fished Corchy's straight through and turned nothing, then hiked down below the ledges and hooked five fish!

We are all very impressed. I pull out the expresso pot and fire up the little stove on the bow, and we sit in the boat or stand around it talking, exulting, getting something we need out of the cooler or the dry box or our vests, doffing sweaters, untying wind knots, tying on new flies and checking points and knots. The sun is nearly up. It has been an excellent morning and I strike up a quick plan to finish it off. Mike and Don will work through the water on this shore while I take Kenny across with me. The wind is kicking up pretty good now. I have to push on the oars to get us along.

We pull in before long and look out on the water. I stand up on the deck over the bow and Kenny is on the cooler and we can see how it is a natural for the fish to come in here. It is shoulder water again out of the main channel, with good structure and speed. It dawns on me how much of that type of water I fish. We can see where the fish move onto the ledges and the oily swirls over the rocks where they hold. I sit down and rummage through the cooler for something to drink while Kenny wades into position.

I watch him cast under the wind. The trick is to lay it on the water before the wind gets hold of it. Kenny is good, it is obvious:

no wasted motions, nothing underdone. He moves along the substrate in a solid three-point stance with his staff. He one-hands the rod well. He and Mike fish a lot together. It shows.

Kenny hooks one here at the very bottom of the run and it is a small fish; I see it jump, but it takes off like a bullet and spools Kenny and snaps his leader, accelerating quickly in the heavy water and the sound is like a pistol shot in the morning air. Across the river the late morning wind has whipped up a couple of twisters along the dusty road. There are black cattle sprinkled like pepper across the face of the hills, high above them enormous stanchions of steel support the power lines from the dams along the Columbia. We are approaching civilization again. Looking due north the mountains of Washington rise above the canyon. Then I see Mike and Don sitting on the river bank in the sun immediately across from us, watching. They'd seen Kenny's fish. One of them cups his hands and shouts something unintelligible over at us. They are too far, but the wind has it anyway.

We ferry across to pick them up, then drop the rest of the way to camp. We are into the standard Deschutes fish now, six to eight pounds, pug-nosed. Wild fish run typically seven-to-one hatchery, but the fighting difference is more a question of individual qualities than stock. It is early for the record-class Idaho fish, but there are big fish around. The sun burns overhead. You feel the heat building in the canyon. My mind goes back (as it frequently does) to the men building the railroad here seventy years ago. Then, drifting through a calm stretch we take turns jumping overboard. Underwater it is ice cold and immensely refreshing. The driftboat casts a deep, malignant shadow and for a moment you want to swim away into the light.

Kloan. We set up what we have with us in the shade of the blowing trees along the west bank. When the support raft shows, we all pitch in and set up the kitchen. Then the desert heat drives everyone into lawn chairs in the shallow water in front of camp, or asleep in whatever shade they can find. I decide to bathe in the cold water this morning and wash the sand out of my hair and ears. Afterward I feel like a new man, and Greg and I decide to hike out of camp to explore an old apricot orchard in the hills above camp. The breeze is hot through the dry grass above the river. We tour the old orchard and return to camp, disappointed. The apricots were small and unthinkably sour. We had been thinking pie.

> *Deschutes/August 11th: Sitting on the grass bank of camp bringing the journal up to date. Mike and Jim Billings work the Bathtub Hole and the Cabin Hole in front of me. Jim is from Augusta, Maine, runs a sheet metal shop there in his spare time, fishes Key West once a year for tarpon and bonefish. It is his first trip to the Deschutes and he compares the summer steelhead favorably to his beloved 'bones.'*
>
> *Don went across with Gordy. Kenny hiked downstream to fish the Green Light Hole (a real greyhound). Greg is doing dishes in the kitchen directly behind me. Gordy's boat hooked eleven fish this morning in Lockit!*
>
> *Home late tomorrow. Tie up some skating patterns this weekend. Remember sun block, and quiz Randall again about the island immediately upstream.*

"So what's open tonight?" Greg calls over my shoulder.

"Well, you could drag my boat up and go across and hike up past the point, but its kind of late for that. Or you could go upstream here and fish the Ass Hole."

We have a good laugh, as always, at this.

The Ass Hole is a fast, pea-gravelled run by the ruins of the old bridge, upstream. Got its name from a guy from Harvard I had down once. I get up grinning, remembering, and put my journal away and dig a cold green apple out of the ice water at the bottom of the Igloo.

"That's a good bet," I said. "And you could check out if those pools along the base of . . . "

The click of a reel grabs our attention; someone's hooked up. It's Mike in the Cabin Hole. I see his rod pulled to the surface in a staccato of surges as his drag slips line. We see a fish jump across the river.

"Did you see that?" Greg says.

"You don't think that was his fish?"

But there is no one on the other side.

Mike's rod never makes it above horizontal. It is over in seconds. Mike and Greg and I exchange glances. Mike grins sheepishly, reeling in his line. It is a good feeling for a guide, having a man at his threshold.

I go back and help Greg with the cleaning, now that he is about done. He grouches good-naturedly at me. I punch him a couple of times in his thick, boatsman's arms.

"Well, Kohn, the fish aren't going to swim into camp looking for you."

"Okay," he says. "Build this," and hands me the coffee pot.

While I make a pot of coffee, Jimmy hooks up directly in front of camp. He has a bird's nest he is furiously trying to pick out; we hear him cussing. I shake my head: "lightning-like," most definitely. But ten minutes later he's hooked up again. The fish is holding straight out.

"Now what?" he shouts in to me.

I wade out barefoot to join him. Jimmy is all smiles. He knows what to do; he just wants to share the fish with someone. After an excellent fight he has it in front of me. I put on my cotton butcher's glove and wade carefully into position while I cup my sunglasses tightly with my hands to see.

I enjoy tailing big fish (nearly a sport in its own right). Like a raptor, I find the fish in a slow frame beside me and dive my hand quickly into the water and have a grip on its wrist. There is a momentary, desperate flurry of energy. I cradle it gently with my hand under its belly and bring up its black and silver flank. Then Jim comes over and slips his fly from the corner of its mouth. It is a beautiful fish. I work it in the current for a moment before releasing it. It is bright, strong.

Out of nowhere a voice calls out from shore. "Haven't seen a hatchery fish all day myself." It is a fisherman in hip boots and cartoon hat. "Don't feel bad," he says.

We won't, I assure him. It doesn't matter to us if it is a hatchery fish or a wild fish. I don't count its fins or measure its dorsal rays to determine its fate. Hell, I'd forgotten to look.

*Deschutes/August 11th (midnight again): Sleeping on board tonight. Always a hassle sleeping out here, moving things around, building the lounge up with one leg on the cooler and one on the dry-well, trying not to drop anything overboard in the dark and wading ashore to pee. It's nice on the water though. The boat is swinging free in a shallow pocket directly off camp, and the wind's softened. I can hear the gas lantern hissing overhead on the handles of the oars I've lashed together.*

*Poked around with the flashlight earlier. Saw the shape of something big on the edge of the light a moment, then it was gone. Sometimes the steelhead come in close at night; we've seen them before. Then Kenny waded out to visit and brought a bottle of Glenfiddich. Said he's had a wonderful trip, that they will all be back again next year. Great bunch of guys, these guys. Sometimes I wonder who should be paying who.*

*Then, hanging over the gunnel, we netted some bugs; several black stonefly and mayfly nymphs, a couple lime-green Ryacophila larva. We found a fry stationed behind a rock and speculated on the little guy's response to an upstream versus a downstream mend, a dead drift versus a swing or a lift. Research.*

*Not a sound from camp now. I'm about to turn in too. By pull-out tomorrow I suspect we'll have hooked over fifty fish between us. Heck of a way to start a season. Gordy's going across early tomorrow to beat the sleds, then dropping to Wagenblast to try and get in there. That's too much like shopping Bean's the week before Christmas; I remember the Christmas I worked there. We'll sit on what we've got.*

Everyone looking forward to the rapids tomorrow, a tonic to the fish-sated, blistered, libidinal likes of us. We have Gordon's Ridge and Colorado and Rattlesnake — 2+, 3, 4 — a white-water crescendo . . . it occurs to me too, that each night in camp has become a little stronger, a little wilder, building on a crescendo of its own. A bright, demonstrative group. Tonight, for example, we kicked around the significance of $E = MC^2$ (in laymen's terms, of course), and the pros and cons of mating for life. Then Kenny and Mike performed this great Irish skit and had everyone in stitches. What it is, I think, is a quality of homogeneity that comes over everyone out here. Gradually, the posturing falls away and there are no more guides or doctors or 'sports' — only fishermen.

# The Beaverkill

## Roderick Haig-Brown

I have never returned to the Beaverkill, though I shall. I have been there only once in my life, but that once felt like a return, as I think it must to any North American fly fisherman. For this, after all, is the true cradle of the sport on our continent. We have all heard of it and read of it, and we all owe a great deal to the men who have fished it and to some who fish it still — to Theodore Gordon, Louis Rhead, Edward Hewitt, George La Branche, Jack Atherton and Sparse Grey Hackle, to name only a few of them.

It is a little stream, dancing brightly out of the timbered Catskills in New York State to its junction with the Willowemoc at Roscoe. From the Junction on it is a big stream, but still a trout stream, a stream a man can cast across and wade around in comfort; and it flows through pleasant farm lands. It is heavily fished, I suppose — it must be, with a name so famous in a state so populous. It is artificially stocked each year with tiny fish. It has largely lost its brook trout, and most of the introduced rainbows that Theodore Gordon wondered about and finally approved of. But the European brown trout is there and in charge. Some of the little fish spawned by the hatchery trucks or planted by the clubs of the upper river manage to evade anglers and survive the heat of summer and the ice of winter. Holdovers, wise and cautious, they may well survive another season and another, to become fish of minor legend and make worthwhile sport for the faithful who try from "fine and far off."

I may as well admit I have never really fished the Beaverkill. But I was there on opening day a year or two back with Ed Zern of *To Hell with Fishing* and Bill Naden, President of the Brooklyn Fly Fishers, the oldest club on the upper reaches. Ed and I came out to Doug Bury's Antrim Lodge at Roscoe on the banks of the Willowemoc on the evening of April twelfth, the day before opening. Ed wanted me to see and feel the mood of opening day, and it was there already as fishermen from all over gathered in the bar at the Lodge. Everyone knew everyone. Everyone was relaxed about the prospects of fishing, which were plainly less than good, but stirred by the pleasures of reunion, the sense of taking part in this special occasion that had been shared in the past by so many of the great names of fly fishing, by so many friends and, often enough, by fathers and grandfathers, uncles and brothers and sons. It was not hard for me, a simple soul from the far west, where I may still find a new trout stream tomorrow, to feel the mood and be impressed by it. We also have our openings, our reunions, our memories of those who fished before us in many of the same places; but we cannot boast a tradition of such power and authority.

Ed and I went out after a while into the clear, cold night to exercise Ed's big Labrador. There was frost on the grass and the roofs, ice on the puddles; a high moon lighted the riffles of the Willowemoc above the highway bridge and the little town was very quiet after the brightness and talk of Doug Bury's bar.

"There won't be any fishing to speak of," Ed told me, echoing the conviction of nearly everyone we had spoken to inside. "But we'll move up and down the river, crack a bottle or two and talk with a lot of old friends."

I believed him and looked forward happily to the prospect. But I couldn't help hoping there might just be one of those sparse winter hatches of pale dulls, a big wise fish, relaxed by his winter of security, rising to them, and myself within range.

Bill Naden joined us early the next morning, and we went downstream at first, all the way to the East Branch of the Delaware, where some of the big browns winter over. The air temperature was 38, the water a discouraging 34. From time to

time snow flurries whirled across the brown faces of the hills
and settled into the valley. Plenty of fishermen were at work,
though the stream certainly was not crowded except at a few
favorite pools where optimistic fishermen lined both sides only
eight or ten feet apart, fly-men and spinners crossing lines in
the same hope that I had briefly held the night before — that
some leviathan, off his guard, might stir from bottom and make
a mistake, or else that a hungry hatchery yearling would accept
all easy offering.

A few, very few, fish were being taken, and those mostly
around six or eight inches. "This is opening day," Bill reminded
me. "It doesn't mean much except that. Half of these fellows
won't show up on the stream again all year and most of the
others won't bother after they think the hatchery fish are used
up. The real fishing here is in the summer and fall. You can
always find a few good fish feeding then if you know the river;
and there's a chance of something really big occasionally."

"Some of the big ones move back up from the East Branch
when the water warms up," Ed said. "You get some nice
hatches at times too."

"Don't any big fish hold over up here?"

"Sure," said Bill. "Some do. Shouldn't be surprised if there's
one or two up under our dam on the club water now."

Another snow flurry came down on us then and Bill said:
"Let's go and take a quick look at the upper reaches, then get
back to the club and have some lunch."

Above its junction with the Willowemoc, the Beaverkill is
quite small, a mountain stream rather than a valley stream,
with steep slopes running up from its banks in most places —
most pleasant slopes, covered by deciduous trees and a few
conifers, with rhododendrons growing wild in the leaf mold
under them. The trees were not yet leafed and the water was
low, almost as I imagined it would be in summertime, with
great piles of ice pans in places along the banks and the trunks
of waterside trees scarred by the tearing of ice in the break-up. I
could see it was not altogether a friendly place for fish to
winter over. But there were plenty of good pools and since
much of the water is privately owned, by clubs or individuals,
a good deal of valuable improvement work has been done. We

saw few fishermen, but once, where the road passed close to a good pool, a nice trout of about twelve inches rose smoothly — to a snowflake, as nearly as we could judge.

The Brooklyn Club was founded in 1895 and has its headquarters in a tumbledown farmhouse far older than that. One ancient angler was dozing, glass in hand, in a deep chair before a huge fire in a huge fireplace. Ed suggested he must be thawing out after a morning in the stream; Bill considered it more likely he had braved only the depths of his chair and been overcome by them since breakfast. We talked in whispers and took on a little warmth ourselves while sorting out rods and gear to go out after lunch.

There was a flutter of sunshine, quickly lost in gray cloud as we started out. There was no possible doubt it was a wetfly day and we were content to tie on wet flies — fairly large streamer patterns at that. We fished the Home Pool, the Twin Rocks and one or two other attractive pools or corners without result, then came to the dam in a minor blizzard that completely hid the far bank. Bill told me he had little doubt there would be a big fish or two spending the last days of his winter's rest somewhere in the deep water under the lip of the dam.

I was more than ready to believe him and went out with fine confidence into the smooth glide of water that slid into the little fall over the wall of rocks. The backward fold of current at the foot of the fall sucked the line down nicely and I could imagine the fly hovering and darting enticingly down in the sheltered water near the bottom. Surely some big brown trout would be hungry down there, surely he must know he would feel better with a nice little minnow firmly down in his stomach; after all, the fish had to start feeding sometime and this could be the moment. So I worked very faithfully with the snow on my face and my eyes half closed to it; but it was not the time and we went back to the Clubhouse fishless, to admire the outlines of splendid *Fontinalis* and *Gairdneri* and *Trutta* that decorated the walls. The ancient angler still slept in his chair, the fire still glowed and we needed warmth.

Surely fly fishers are the most disregarded of men. This river, of all North American rivers, is the shrine of their sport. In this and others in the Catskills the North American fly fisher began his serious affairs. "For over a hundred years," wrote Theodore Gordon, more than fifty years ago, "the valley of the Beaverkill has been celebrated for its beauty and the river for its trout." To these streams the tradition crossed the Atlantic, to be steadily reinforced and developed by continuing exchanges between fishermen of the old world and the new.

From these streams, and especially from the Beaverkill, the old traditions, reinforced by the new, went out to the rest of the continent to be tried and used and still further adapted until they fitted the needs of each new place. Surely it is time for the Beaverkill to be set aside as the fly fisherman's shrine forever. It should be left for fly fishermen, and fly fishermen only. Some thought should be given to the possibilities of restoration. Is it too warm for the eastern brook trout, too heavily fished, unsuitable in some other way? If so, what chance would there be of counteracting the difficulty and bringing the fish back as Daniel Webster and Frank Forester and so many others knew them?

Failing this, there is more than enough to be said for the brown trout provided he is reasonably abundant and of respectable size, say from ten inches up — and of course reserved for the fly fisherman so that the craftier individuals have at least an even chance to last out a few seasons and grow to an impressive size.

The river has been tidied up and its banks are now fairly well-protected from the activities of garbage dumpers and trash throwers, thanks to the writings of Sparse Grey Hackle in the magazine *Sports Illustrated*. But this seems hardly enough. Isn't there room for some great gesture by fly fishermen all over the United States and Canada to have this one river set aside as a perpetual monument to the sport — a monument that many might never see, but all should know!

After all, it shouldn't be such a tremendous task. The stream still has most of its natural beauty. The valley still has its great fly-tiers and conservationists like the Darbees and the Dettes. It still has its magic name. Above all it still has its faithful few, sons and grandsons and by now even great-grandsons of those who originally fished there, as well as those who have found it more recently. A Derbyshire fisherman wrote me just the other day: "I have recently fished Walton and Cotton's stretch of the Dove. The Fishing Hut and the cut-off tree trunk for lunch outside are still there."

Is it too much to ask, for all of North America, just one stream so dedicated and protected forever?

# Fishing in Hemingway Country

Jerry Dennis

Anyone who spends much time outdoors in Michigan is likely to find himself crossing the trails of legends. Many of the most impressive trails tend to follow trout streams, and to have been made by one legend in particular, a young fellow from Oak Park, Illinois named Ernest Hemingway. Young Hemingway surveyed much of the best fishing in northern Michigan, and documented it so thoroughly and memorably that on certain waters it is difficult to find a stretch free of literary associations. Consequently, some of us, instead of ignoring legends altogether and just going fishing, end up turning our fishing trips into pilgrimages.

Like many people, I first read Hemingway's short story, "Big Two-Hearted River" in a high school English class. It was no accident, of course: harried instructors learned long ago that they could not keep order in a class forced to plod through *Anna Karenina* or *Jude the Obscure*. What was needed was something short, something compelling, and Hemingway's accessible stories with their compressed, declarative sentences served admirably.

"Big Two-Hearted River" overwhelmed me, partly because I was a trout fanatic, partly because I grew up in northern

Michigan, near rivers the young Hemingway had fished during his summer vacations on Walloon Lake. Although bothered that Hemingway did not specify the size and type of trout Nick Adams caught, I became determined to fish the Two-Hearted with live grasshoppers on a fly rod, eat peaches from a can, and snuff mosquitos on the side of my tent with a flaring match. It would be years before I learned how difficult (and dangerous) that could be, and before I learned that Hemingway had duped us with his Two-Hearted River title. The story was about the Fox, not the Two-Hearted. Hemingway was a liar.

By now the Fox/Two-Hearted question creates little debate, but in those days it was a matter of some controversy. Graduate students made it the subject of dissertations, and some literary sleuths were said to have travelled to Seney, retraced as closely as possible Nick Adam's course over the rolling country north of town, and concluded that it was impossible for him to have hiked in one day to the actual Two-Hearted — which is located some twenty miles north of the Fox, and flows in the opposite direction, north to Lake Superior.

John Voelker, the U.P. trout laureate and author (as Robert Traver) of such classic books as *Anatomy of a Murder*, *Trout Madness* and *Trout Magic*, addressed the problem with characteristic good humor in a wonderful essay titled, "Hemingway's Big Two-Hearted Secret." In it he argues that Hemingway merely did what any sensible angler would: disguised the name of a favorite trout stream to keep the hordes away.

The debate may have been ended for good when Carlos Baker, in his 1969 biography, reported that Hemingway explained the name change was made, "not from ignorance or carelessness but because Big Two-Hearted River is poetry."

It was not poetry so much as the urge to catch big trout that sent me on my pilgrimage to the Fox. I was living in Marquette, passing my weekdays in college classrooms and libraries and spending my week-ends and holidays exploring nearby rivers and creeks. In the library I learned of Hemingway's trip to the Fox River in 1919, the year he returned home wounded from Italy. He and his friends Al Walker and John Pentecost camped for a week along the Fox, near the town of Seney, once a rough-and-tumble lumber center famed for its brothels and bars, that had been destroyed by forest fires in 1891 and 1895, and was a virtual ghost town by 1919. Hemingway and friends caught nearly two hundred brook trout that week, including several that reached fourteen and fifteen inches. Hemingway, describing the trip in a letter, wrote that one fish broke his line and was the "biggest trout I've ever seen . . . and felt like a ton of bricks."

Early on a humid Saturday in June I set out to hitch-hike the seventy-five miles to Seney and the Fox River. I wore a backpack loaded with my sleeping bag, tent, food, and chest waders, and carried my fly rod and a paperback edition of Hemingway's Nick Adams stories. The book was a wise choice, for I would do far more reading than fishing that weekend.

The Fox even today has a reputation for brook trout of a size rarely encountered in the United States. Fish of fifteen to twenty inches are taken with fair regularity, primarily by locals with a knack for drifting nightcrawlers through the deep pools downstream from M-28. Some of those trout — wide-bodied beauties with their brilliant, jewel-bright spots highlighted with hobby paint — have been mounted and hung on the walls of area service stations and tackle shops. Ask attendants where those fish were caught and they're likely to avoid your eyes and mumble the names of remote Canadian provinces, but don't believe them for a moment.

It took most of the morning to reach Seney, in three rides, including an unforgettable thirty-five-mile hitch from Munising to Seney through the infamous Seney Stretch — twenty-three miles of straight-as-an-arrow highway through wetlands and tamarack thickets — in a pickup driven by a skinny, wild-eyed old man just coming off a three-day drinking binge. Apologizing for the condition of his truck cab, he proceeded to tell stories about his youth as a lumberjack in the Upper Peninsula. He had once walked the twenty-three miles of the Seney Stretch, at night, after missing his ride back to lumber camp at the end of a weekend of recreation in town. He tried to hitch-hike, he recalled, but in those days traffic was rare as pocket-money (his words) and he was forced to walk the entire distance, arriving in camp barely in time to eat breakfast and follow the crew to the woods.

Seney today is a crossroads village composed of a service station or two, and several restaurants, motels and taverns strung out along M-28. The bridge over the Fox River is a quarter-mile west of most of that industry, as if the town, when it was rebuilt after the fires of the 1890s, was shifted slightly askew by a surveyor's miscalculation. There are no signs of fire now, but if you travel north parallel to the river along County Road 450, you will eventually reach an area of uplands known as the Kingston Plains, where treeless, rolling hills are dotted with the dried and silvered stumps of ancient pines, many still charred at the edges from forest fires.

I had expected the river to be clear and lively, bubbling over bright cobblestone. Upstream would be a stretch of meadow water where large trout rose to grasshoppers and, beyond it, the river disappeared into a dark swamp that promised even larger trout.

Instead the Fox is small, passes through thickets of tag alders and is prone to fallen trees. The water is discolored, a blend of silt and swamp drainings, and flows with little vitality over sand bottom. Several days of rain had raised and muddied the water, and I walked through the wet, waist-high grasses below the bridge to get a better look at it.

I grew up in northern Michigan, I know biting insects intimately, but I have never seen mosquitos like those that rose from the weeds and grasses along the Fox River that day. Larger and more aggressive than the bugs of ordinary experience, they surrounded me in a whining, frenzied, desperate search for blood. Repellent was useless. Any insects that might have been repelled were forced against me by those behind. Even when I sprayed the aerosol directly at them they scarcely altered their flight. They absorbed the poison and developed genetic immunity instantly.

Panicked, I ran north, upstream, in the direction Nick Adams hiked. But every mosquito in the area was alerted and there was no outrunning them. I met a man wearing a netting over his head and carrying an impressively stout bait-casting rod. I asked in passing how the fishing was. Terrible, he said.

That decided it. I turned around, ran back to the highway,

and caught a ride west with a young family in a Toyota. They were from Wisconsin and had been camping near Tahquamenon Falls. I squeezed into the back seat with the two sons, whose faces were swollen with insect bites. The parents wanted local color. I told them the old man's tale about the Seney Stretch, and explained that the river they had just crossed was the model for the famous Hemingway story, "Big Two- Hearted River." The information seemed to disappoint them.

They let me out along the Lake Superior shoreline near Munising. I set my tent on the beach in the perpetual, bug-free wind, and passed the remainder of the weekend reading Hemingway's stories and considering the folly of angling pilgrimages. I never uncased my fly rod.

# Salmon, Cider and Oranges

## Randolph Osman

One bright morning in Madrid's huge San Pedro market, I saw ten and twelve pound Atlantic Salmon, chrome-bright slabs on ancient marble dressing palettes. Two men were cleaning the fish and talking in Castillian Spanish, but the accent was from somewhere else, perhaps another province, perhaps a dialect. I introduced myself, complimented them on the salmon, and asked where they were from.

"From Asturias," was the proud reply. "The salmon are from our boats in Gijón. We bring them down here overnight. That way they are fresh everyday." It wasn't hard to elicit descriptions and praise for this land of green valleys, misty rock-lined coasts, and rushing rivers. "You should go there, señor, you will like it." I did and they were right.

Northern Spain is a fly fishing paradise where green mountains, separated by magnificent Atlantic salmon rivers, create the backdrop for thousands of miles of rocky coastline bordering the Cantabrian Sea to the north. The bulk of these great salmon rivers courses through the province of Asturias in the north-center of the Iberian peninsula. Their names ring like phonetic chime — the Eo (pronounced "eey-yo"), the Esva, the Sella, the Deva, the Navia, and the Narcea.

An art historian and museum curator specializing in Spanish medieval art, I had traveled a good bit in Spain, but never to the Cantabrian coast. I had planned to visit the ancient architectural shrines along pilgrimage routes leading to the 11th century church of Santiago de Compostela in the extreme northwest of the peninsula. I would take notes and photos at Santiago, but I was secretly determined to visit the Narcea River and the legendary salmon fly tyer, Belarmino Martínez, who lives in Santa Catalina, a tiny village on the fabled river's lower stretches. As for fishing, I could only hope.

The Narcea River winds down through the Cantabrian Cordillera mountains past forested valleys, over a lush coastal plain of farms and towns, spilling eventually into the bay of Saint Stephen between Cudillero and Avilés. It links the ancient mountain village of Cangas del Narcea with the Bay of Biscay and the Cantabrian Sea. Ancient ports, like Gijón, have seen Asturians trading with the British, the Danes and the Welsh for hundreds of years. No doubt the Asturians and their northern neighbors have also traded tales of their salmon rivers, and their favorite flies, for generations.

The annual inception of the great medieval pilgrimages parallels the annual migration of the Atlantic salmon in this region. In fact salmon fishing season begins right around Easter. Salmon, like pilgrims, return to their sources of nourishment, acting out nature's rebirth in the spring. When the April rains have made the rivers fat and have melted the mountain snows, in Chaucer's words, "Thanne longen folk to go on pilgrimages." And indeed they still do. Some take flyrods!

Meals, like bullfights, are serious business in Spain, only slightly less ritualized than High Mass on Easter Sunday. I chose an esteemed restaurant in Santiago de Compostela, where I discovered a very distinguished and tweedy septuagenarian who looked like — and was — a retired physician. He asked in the best "Oxbridge" English if I enjoyed the local Ribeira wine, then he proceeded to pour me a glass from his own bottle. He wasn't British, however, but Swiss. He told me about the prized Galician scallop (or Viera) served singly in the same familiar fluted shell worn by pilgrims to Santiago for more than a thousand years. It was just a hunch, but I asked if he might by chance be a fly fisher. He must have noticed my nose twitching. He mentioned his favorite river, the Rio Eo, which divides Galicia from Asturias. He grinned at the rhyme in Spanish and soon was rambling enthusiastically about his yearly trips to the legendary Eo. He was to meet his guide there tomorrow afternoon. They fished with a fourteen foot, two-handed cane rod. He described his longing to cast a floating line across deep pools and to wait for a gentle tug before the pool would burst into action.

Did he know of Belarmino Martínez? Yes, he thought so, wasn't there an article about him published recently in one of the Swiss fly fishing magazines? I reached into my shirt pocket and produced a couple of Belarmino's Atlantic Salmon flies. One was called a "Narcea River," tied on a #2 hook. Dr. Hans Klimt examined it, stroking and smoothing the carefully married wing feathers.

"Have you seen him tie one of these?" he asked.

"No," I replied, "but I hope to meet him and perhaps watch him work."

"So you are going to meet Señor Martínez, and visit his river?"

He turned the Narcea River pattern over again and again. "This is exquisite, one of the finest I've seen. Like a little Spanish dancer, everything in exact proportion, so carefully designed."

"You keep it," I said, "its the least I can do in exchange for learning about Ribeira wine and the luscious viera."

Klimt prepared to leave. As he rose, he leaned forward and wrote "Cangas del Narcea" on a slip of paper. "I may go there," he said, "and after that perhaps to Cornellana further down the river."

After the leisurely meal and treasured conversation, I felt entirely at home. The proverbial bond between fly fishers seemed as strong as ever. We went out into the April rain and shook hands. On the way to my hotel, I said a prayer to the Virgin of the Sea (assuming there was one), thanking her for the scallops and Ribeira wine, and invoking her powers to keep the Swiss doctor from slipping on an Asturian river rock. I wanted to see him again — to absorb his knowledge of Asturian rivers, to learn the graceful dance with the long cane rod. But he was headed for the Eo to meet his guide. And I was going to the Narcea, hoping to meet Belarmino Martínez.

I planned the trip from Santiago to the Narcea following a circuitous route through the high interior of Asturias. The closer I got to the headwaters of the legendary salmon rivers, as I drove north into the Asturian mountains, the less ignorant of fly fishing were people in cafés, hotels, and sporting goods stores. One shop sold hardware, olives, sausage and soap. I asked my by now ritualized question about the Narcea, salmon flies and Belarmino. The proprietor produced some flies in little plastic envelopes with the name "B. Martinez" printed on the back. I bought them. Farther on I met a group of fishermen in a café. One was "in uniform," a rumpled wool khaki affair with a randomly sewn-on official patch that identified him as a "Guarda," an official government river guard stationed to monitor the numerous public access points for fishing. While not as inaccessible as most European rivers, Spanish rivers are private property, save those designated locations where citizens and foreigners with the appropriate licenses can fish legally. He knew Belarmino, and wrote down directions to the nearby town of Cornellana on the Narcea River. "Go to this café and ask about Belarmino, they will tell you how to find him."

In Cornellana, still high in the interior mountains, about twenty-five kilometers from the coast, I was clearly in salmon fishing territory. Little hotels and cafés sported long cane rods, waders, creels, nets, lures, hooks, and flies. The café in question was obviously centered around salmon fishing. Men at small tables wore hip-boots and waders. The back room was piled from floor to ceiling with boxes of everything — reels, leaders, boots, and flies. There were hundreds of Atlantic salmon patterns. Most were from England, via the ubiquitous "casa Hardy". They appeared to be export versions, with bulky heads, uneven ribbing, not what I was used to from Hardy's. I fondled some of Belarmino's, so obviously superior to the others.

Outside the café the sun was slipping behind the cover of trees on a hill above the town. Across the road an ancient vaulted stone bridge arched over the water surface. I walked to the middle of the bridge and watched the river. Swallows (those airborne, wingéd trout) were intercepting flies in mid-air. It was too early for the bats. Across the river in a small hamlet, bells chimed from the 12th century monastery church of San Salvador buried in a web of amber-colored buildings that made me think of Cézanne paintings — all angular and linked together by the light of the setting sun.

The river was deep and quiet here. It cut a sharp edge along the bank, as it moved gently and rhythmically past lush green-leaved branches that touched the water, were held and stretched downstream, snapping back in place like spring-set snares. There were tight curls in the surface of the river, like swirls of colored marble in the columns of weathered Roman temples. Farther down, the long pool formed a tail-out as the water hastened into riffles, turning and sweeping into a swift current as it disappeared around an elbow bend. A moment ago in the distance, across the valley, a herd of sheep moved slowly toward town. Now I could see them ambling single file down the main street of the village.

The swallows were taking what I thought were caddis flies with such abandon I could actually hear their wings slice through the air. It is said the greatest flattery to a fly tyer is to have a swallow chase the fly through the air. If a bat chases it, even better. There is no more discriminating connoisseur of artificial insects than the bat. Spanish bats are no exception, I thought. I looked for salmon holding somewhere in the current, but the water was dark, nearly black. The surface was a shiny mirror showing swallows and bats, but no salmon. I knew what they should look like. They would be lined up close together on the river bottom, barely moving in the current like loaves of Spanish bread lined up on a shelf in a brick oven.

In the twilight I crossed the bridge and slid down a cobblestone embankment to the river's edge. Mesmerized by the dark waters, my mind wandered back through history. It wasn't far from here that Charlemagne, on another river a little to the east, had stopped to quench his thirst during his reconquest of the Iberian Peninsula in the 9th century. It was somewhere in this region too that Charlemagne is believed to have experienced his mystical vision of Santiago (St. James Major). I wondered if Santiago or Charlemagne had crossed the river here. Suddenly I returned to the present with a shock.

The surface of the river erupted in a turbulent splash and a bright silver fish the length of my arm leaped and threw water across the tail of the pool, then hit the surface again with a bang like a pistol shot. As the water cleared, I could see the fish holding tenaciously in the current. In the corner of its mouth was a bright spot, a flicker of green and gold in the fading light. The fish dropped back a few yards then moved closer to shore. Again it jumped, arcing like a Saracen sickle-moon, hitting the black water with a sharp crack and disappearing from sight. Within seconds I saw it leap again, the fly still visible in the corner of its mouth. Moments later the pool was silent once more.

The sun finally set behind the bell tower of San Salvador abbey, and a gentle fog began to issue from the surface of the river. The smells of the Asturian mountain night rolled in like an ocean tide as I turned and headed back across the road to a tackle shop and café. There were several small marble-topped tables in front where weathered men in blue berets sat drinking cognac. The image of the salmon with the green-bodied fly in its mouth hung in my mind's eye like a painted icon.

Inside I ordered a plate of mussels in garlic and white wine sauce with a bottle of Ribeira. The wine was a little expensive, slightly exotic for a local café. I savored the mussels, the bread and the Ribeira. I knew it might be a long time before I tasted them again in this way.

I heard the café door open. I looked up and Hans Klimt was standing there. He was wearing a hounds-tooth sport coat and hip boots, his white hair slightly yellowed at the tips. He recognized me and walked over to my table.

"What a pleasant surprise. My American teacher friend, here on the Narcea River. Have you been fishing?"

A second order of mussels was called for ... and another bottle of Ribeira. Klimt told me he had spent a day on the Eo, but the water was high. He decided to try the Narcea which is smaller and drains faster. He thought Cornellana would be perfect. There were numerous "cotos" for access right here. Then he leaned over and confided, "You know, I just played the most beautiful fish. Right there! Just below the bridge. He

surely weighed six kilos. After two jumps he broke off and that
was all."

"And he took your fly," I said flatly.

"Well, no, he took *your* fly, or Señor Martínez' fly — the
beautiful 'Narcea River' with the green body and the teal blue
shoulder."

"That was a lucky fish," I said. Then I explained how I'd
seen a fly in the corner of the fish's mouth below the bridge
only moments ago. Hans was amazed. "You saw the fish, and
the Martínez fly?"

"Well, I saw a fish with a green fly in its mouth." Klimt
nodded in approval. I went on, "Tomorrow I'll be in Právia and
Santa Catalina, maybe I'll meet Belarmino Martínez. Maybe I'll
get another of his exquisite salmon flies."

An hour later we left two huge mounds of shiny black
mussel shells piled on thick white plates. We paid the bill and
bid good night. I crossed the street to my hotel. From my room
I could see the outline of the bridge, and in the background the
tower of the church of San Salvador. I imagined salmon lined
up along the gravel bed of the river, their bodies undulating
silently under the moon. Small green branches swept the river
gently from the overhanging foliage on the banks. Then I
stumbled to bed and to sleep. Tomorrow promised to be
another long day.

Late the next afternoon at the tabac in Právia, an ageless,
sturdy woman in a house-dress took me by the hand and led
me next door where a teenage girl sold ice cream. "Pili," she
said, "take this man to see Belarmino. I will tend the store."

Belarmino Martinez could have been a lawyer or an
accountant or a teacher. Slight of build, athletic and grey-
haired, he wore a plain sport shirt and rimless glasses. He
asked if I planned to fish his river, the Narcea. I explained that I
was only there for a few days, that I had really come to meet
Belarmino Martínez, perhaps to watch him tie some salmon
flies, to see the ancient churches in the area, and to learn about
Asturias. Belarmino smiled, thought a minute, then offered to
take me with him to the river.

"Can you go tomorrow? I have boots and a fly rod, and of
course I have flies," he smiled. "I will call a good friend to

come here from Oviedo in the morning. We will go together
and you can learn our way of casting the rod and the fly,
because I think it is different from your American way."

Like fly fishers the world over, Belarmino is reverent
toward his rivers. He offered abundant hospitality and told me
ancient legends about the Narcea Valley.

The next morning was bright and crisp. I was pleased and
excited to have a chance on the Narcea. Manuel Félix Díaz
Álvarez, President of the Asturian Sport Fishing Association
arrived by car from Oviedo, half an hour away. The three of us
drove across the valley to a field decorated with conical
haystacks. We donned hip boots, vests and waders and
marched through morning dew to a cutbank pool at a bend in
the Narcea. In a noble gesture of courtesy, Belarmino set up his
nine-foot graphite rod and allowed me the first cast. I began to
feed line and to make several false casts, putting out enough
line to allow the fly to sink deeply. After two or three heroic
double-hauls, Manuel Díaz could endure it no longer.

"Please let me demonstrate how we cast." And he threw
out sixty feet of line in one graceful sweep with his own
twelve-foot, double-handed glass rod. "You see, just one clean
sweep — like dancing." Then ensued a conversation about
"short" American flyrods, ubiquitous false casts, much-touted
"line speed," the American philosophy and technology of
power and long casts as ends in themselves. The Spaniards had
fished with and observed Americans casting short high density
graphite rods achieving remarkable distance through powerful
backcasts and enormous rod strengths. Díaz had also fished in
England and Scandinavia, and he was not bashful in his
applause for the European long rod and its graceful cast. He
demonstrated with one sweeping pick-up of line from the
water and a single rolling loop to the head of a pool. He
emphasized that the aesthetic qualities of the long rod and the
single cast far out-weighed the rapid-fire, multiple false-casts,
feeding line through a short, stiff American-style graphite rod.
According to Díaz, his casting was simply "more civilized."
Indeed, I have friends who cast regularly on Oregon's famed
Deschutes River with fourteen-foot glass rods and argue "style
and aesthetics" in defense of a single false cast or a roll cast.

The morning slipped by without a swirl in the pool. Two fishermen passed us and exchanged familiar greetings. This was private water, accessible only to friends of the landlord. I watched the two fishermen with their long cane rods disappear around a bend in the river headed upstream. Like most others on this river, they made casts with a single overhand motion, usually with only one backcast, or right from the end of a previous swing, using a single roll cast. One of the men, named Pepe, had just moved out of sight, when I heard him exclaim "Oye, Salmón!" I knew he had hooked one.

Leaving Belarmino and Manuel, I ran upstream and saw Pepe perched on a rock outcropping, the long cane rod arched high above his head, the line at forty-five degrees from the rod tip, the leader buried in a swift stretch of water. Then the salmon broke the surface, cartwheeled once and dug in again. Above the river a rugged "horreo," or grain storage bin, hand-hewn from granite, stood like a medieval sentinel, its squat stone legs rising above the river like truncated Greek temple columns. It cast an ominous reflection, shading the pool where the salmon held tenaciously.

Pepe brought the fish closer to shore; his friend reached out with a net and the battle was ended. A bright silver hen lay quietly on the river rocks. Pepe clubbed it once and knelt to remove his fly from the corner of the mandible. He examined the fish again and exclaimed with surprise, "what's this?". Then he removed a second fly from the fish's mouth and held it up for all to see. It was a #2 green body fly with a teal blue shoulder, an orange tail and a mottled brown wing. Pepe recognized the fly and the pattern. He had seen many Martínez Narcea River patterns before. He also knew I was a "guest" on his river. He handed the fly to me and said "this, sir, is a fly tied by Señor Martínez, our country's finest. We just passed him fishing down below with a friend."

I smiled secretly. "Yes, I know. Thank you for this beautiful salmon fly," I replied humbly. I could hardly believe it! I had read somewhere that Narcea River salmon often wandered haphazardly up various small tributaries anxiously searching for their natal stream, sometimes returning to the main stem of the river to try all over again. I wondered if I would see Hans

Klimt again to return him the fly I was sure he had lost to Pepe's fish. I decided to continue on upstream and return to Manuel and Belarmino later. Maybe I too would have some luck.

Further on there was another ancient stone bridge, this one with double arches. The central pier of the bridge split the river almost down the center. Two deep canyons of dark water flowed on either side of the pier and then spread out into a broad tongue creating classic riffles over a shallow tail of yellow gravel. Broken water in the center of the deeper part of the tongue looked like a good holding place for migrating salmon. I headed up and made several casts to the deeper water at the base of the bridge, planning to interest a fish when the fly entered the broken water. As the line swung and tightened, I saw my fly cut the surface, describing a semi-circle and repeating the shape of the Roman arch reflected from the bridge. In Alaska I had learned from a veteran guide to move two steps at a time in one direction, making a cast at each move, covering the whole river in a series of overlapping curves. I moved along, following the reflected pattern of the Roman bridge, casting in repeated arcs.

Moving under the bridge, over somebody's muskrat trap, and around a gravel bend, I approached yet another stone bridge. This one framed the river beautifully. In the distance was a romanesque church with a rusticated stone tower capped by a tiny belfry. The belfry itself had two arches per side. Suddenly the bells erupted into a clamorous symphony of chimes, signalling it was 6 p.m.

Evening had approached all too quickly. Dinner in rural Asturias is served early by metropolitan Madrid standards. The treasured smells of olive oil, garlic, and baked fabadas (the classic Asturian large white stewed lima bean) began to seep down into the valley of the Narcea from the kitchens perched on the banks above. The sun was very low. The river lay flat now, unmoved by the evening events of the town around it. A heavy-set woman wrapped in anonymous layers of black clothing weilded a gnarled stick to guide a fat sow across the bridge and through a garden gate, disappearing into a maze of ancient stone buildings. As swallows and bats began to appear, I made several more long casts to the cut bank across the river.

I fed line into the drift and hoped my fly went deep enough to attract something. At one point I felt a tug, and adrenalin coursed through my blood. But the fly came back empty and the river ran ceaselessly on.

Looking for a place to climb the bank and regain the road to Santa Catalina, I kept moving ahead — two steps at a time — casting in Roman arcs. On the bank above me, lights flickered. A man about my own age walked a bicycle with a huge loaf of bread tied above the rear wheel. He stopped on the bridge to watch me cast. "Se puede subir?" I asked him, gesturing toward the town. He pointed to a stone walkway behind a tree and I climbed to the road.

I returned to the familiar field with the conical haystacks and to Belarmino and Manuel. Together we headed to a favorite café that served the best local "cidra" (hard apple cider resembling a rich dry dinner wine). On the way I learned that Asturias may be the only part of the world to host three natural delicacies not usually found in the same place. "Salmones, cidra y naranjas," boasted Manuel, "This land has all three," and a sweep of his arm covered the surrounding Narcea Valley all the way to the sea. The warm breezes, cold rivers and fertile soil is a unique combination. I was used to apples and salmon from Oregon and Washington. But the Asturians boast excellent orange trees as well. Summers are long and winters mild. Apples have always been a staple crop, and salmon, of course, have returned to Asturian rivers from time immemorial.

At home, within minutes of the Narcea River, Belarmino ties his flies in his small kitchen which doubles as a fly tying room. The noon meal is finished, the kitchen table is cleared, and fly tying materials are spread out. Belarmino covers the white porcelanized metal table with a green cloth and carefully lays out his feathers. He makes all his tools himself by hand, from spare parts. Even his tying thread is carefully unravelled from discarded women's nylon hose.

Many of his fly patterns are named after Asturian rivers near his home — Deva, Eo, Cares, Navia, Pas, Sella, Narcea. Some are named for the inventor himself — the Martínez Special, the Silver Martínez. He is an unceremonious, matter-of-fact craftsman. As he works, he talks — about dying traditions, about depleted salmon runs, about the tiny 11th century church of Santa Catalina, another important shrine, close to the banks of the Narcea.

Before leaving Asturias, I travelled back to Cornellana, again crossing the ancient stone bridge, climbing down the cobblestone embankment to the river's edge, hoping to relive my previous experience, to see a salmon swirl in the pool. I passed several hours, alternately walking within view of the medieval monastery church of San Salvador, then returning to the elbow bend in the river where the enigmatic salmon had escaped from Hans Klimt carrying Belarmino's Narcea River pattern and delivering it to Pepe, several miles below. I took that fly from my pocket and looked at it. This one has a special history now, I thought. It is linked to its namesake in a special way; it binds together a consummate fly tyer, a legendary river, a treasured friendship, and migration and pilgrimage as a way of life and a means of survival.

Back at home in Oregon I have a large exhibition size (4/0) "Narcea River" salmon fly, a gift from Belarmino Martínez. The body is green, the tail is orange and yellow, the wing a mottled brown. It is sleek and streamlined with a teal blue shoulder. When I look at it, I am reminded again of Asturias, of its farms and green valleys, its orange trees, and of the Narcea river and its steel-blue salmon, a land that, through a thousand years of careful stewardship, can still simultaneously provide its people with salmon, cider and oranges.

# The Platforms of Despair

Ernest Schwiebert

It was unusually cool in northern Europe that summer. The last evening at the Frognerseter Restaurant, there was a soft bluish sea fog that covered the entire fjord, muting the lights of the capital and its circling harbor. The sea fog had drifted into the city itself when I finally started back to the Bristol, its mists filling the narrow streets below the fashionable shops in the Stortingsgata. The lights along the waterfront were surprisingly yellow in the layered mists, and the shipping cranes stood like a flock of sleeping herons.

Frognerseter is a fine restaurant that stands high in the forest-covered Nordmarka hills that surround Oslo. Its excellent cuisine is well known throughout the capital. Its pickled herring and its *gratlaks*, a kind of richly cured salmon served with a dark sauce of mustard and brown sugar and dill, are worth the trip.

Sometimes I spent several hours enjoying its rich food and its unique panorama of the Oslofjord, starting with the herring and cured salmon in its dill sauce. Depending on my moods, that prelude was sometimes followed with crayfish or fresh halibut or char from Hordaland and Telemark. Desert was a simple bowl of cloudberries and sugar, with a small glass of Chateau d'Yquem.

*Årøy*, I thought with excitement as I sampled the wine.

*You're finally getting to fish the Årøy Steeplechase.*

The Årøy has long been talked about with reverence in the salmon-fishing world, and even the legendary Charles Ritz wrote of the river with a touch of awe in his *Fly Fisher's Life*. It was a little like a dream, knowing that I would soon be fishing the Årøy Steeplechase, and with Nicholas Denissoff, the Russian exile who had held the Årøy since 1921.

It was late when I finished my dinner at Frognerseter. The headwaiter brought my change and called a taxi.

"Hotel Bristol," I told the driver.

Our route wound down into the suburbs of Oslo, past the royal palace and its beautiful park, and I changed my mind about the hotel. The taxi driver dropped me at the Teatercafeen, just across the street from the National Theater. Its repertory company had just finished a performance of *Rosmersholm* and the restaurant was filling with the theater crowds. Teatercafeen has high richly decorative ceilings and tall windows hung with heavy purple draperies, like a setting in some film about Moscow or Vienna. It was already crowded with students drinking coffee, and arguing about Ibsen and Kierkegaard and Fellini. Two older men were drinking aquavit and talking politics, and a young man was arguing his theories about Edvard Munch.

The bartender warmed the glass and the cognac was soft and richly aged, and I sat enjoying its bouquet while I eaves-dropped, thinking about the Årøy Steeplechase. When I finished the cognac and finally left the Teatercafeen, I walked thoughtfully back along the Karl Johannsgata toward the Hotel Bristol.

It was difficult to sleep that last night in Oslo, since my head was filled with thoughts of Denissoff and his remarkable river. I stood in the window of my room long after midnight, looking down into the foggy streets. It was almost daylight when I finally fell asleep, thinking about Charles Ritz and the Steeplechase.

"You must see it!" Ritz had gestured excitedly at lunch in New York, his eyes bright and his volatile eyebrows echoing his intensity. "It is like nothing else in the world — and the opportunity to fish the Årøy with Denissoff is like fishing in Valhalla!"

After breakfast I started north in a rented Volvo, winding

down the Oslofjord past Sandvika, and crossing the forested hills into the Tyrifjord country. Beyond the sawmills at Hönefoss, the narrow road wound deep into the mountains that surround the Begnesdalselva, and I stopped in the misting rain to watch its trout rising to a hatch of flies. Fagernes lies in its headwaters, and beyond the steep-walled valley at Vang, the road climbs steadily toward the Sognefjord.

Through the high barrens there, with their lakes and lonely farmsteads and waterfalls, the road finally drops down swiftly toward the Laerdal Valley. Its river gathers itself in its alpine headwaters, in a plunging of wild cataracts among its mossy boulders. Its upper valley is surprisingly gentle in its moods, its currents meandering through lush hayfields and farmsteads of sod-roofed buildings. The river there is thought to offer fine trout fishing, but the Sognefjord country has several of the best salmon fisheries in the world, and a serious angler is seldom distracted by trout on salmon water.

Where the valley grows narrow, the Borgund stave church stands just above the river, its steep gables and free-standing bell tower and intricate roof frames all sheathed in shingles stained with centuries of pitch. Borgund was built in 1150, its timber framework telling us that its architects were probably Viking shipwrights. Its builders still used the dragon's-head ornaments that had earlier graced the prows of Viking longships. Columns and door frames and lintels were all richly carved with a coiling ornamentation that celebrated foliage and stags and serpents. The morning I stopped the churchyard was empty, with no wind stirring in the birches that surround its rubble walls. Ragged clouds hung low over the valley floor, and the mood of the stave church seemed sombre.

Downstream from the churchyard, the river drops into a rocky gorge where several waterfalls stop the salmon migrations upstream. I drove quickly through the winding gorge, past the timber casting platforms at Langhølm and Hunderi, where the beautiful little river flowed swift and smooth. The village of Laerdalsøyri lay ahead in the trees, and I stopped for lunch at the Lindström. Charles Ritz came walking through the flower gardens of the little Victorian hotel as I parked the Volvo across the street.

"Come have lunch with us!" Ritz clasped me by both shoulders. "Creusevaut is already waiting in the dining room."

Ritz and his friend Creusevaut are both dead now, but in those first heady years of peace that followed the Second World War, Pierre Creusevaut was a world champion on the tournament-casting circuit. It was a surprising piece of luck that I had encountered them both at the Lindstöm, and Ritz led me upstairs to its dining room, where Creusevaut had organized a table on the balcony.

Ritz introduced us and took a wineglass from an adjacent table. "Did you arrange some fishing with Denissoff?" He filled the glass with a skilled, rolling stroke of his wrist, and passed it across the table without interrupting his barrage of talk.

"Denissoff offered me three or four days."

"Did he prove difficult?" Ritz continued.

"You predicted that." I smiled.

Creusevaut smiled with amusement, sipped his wine while Ritz accelerated his questions, and sat listening indulgently. "What did Denissoff tell you about the fishing?" Ritz continued his barrage. "Did he charge a lot of money for the entire beat?"

"He told me that the fishing was excellent," I replied, "although he said the Årøy was a little low — and it wasn't cheap!"

"The old robber baron!" Ritz shook his head and laughed. "His fishing has been terrible this past fortnight!"

"There's very little water," Creusevaut added.

"Terrible or not," I accepted more wine gratefully. "You don't get the chance to fish the Steeplechase every day."

"Mais oui!" Ritz agreed.

Ritz led our party to the cold table, which stood in splendour just inside the dining room doors. It held several kinds of brislings in various sauces, and several types of pickled herring. Tiny shrimps covered a huge silver bowl filled with crushed ice, and a gleaming tureen was filled with a delicate asparagus soup. There were platters of fresh sausages and fried halibut and boiled salmon netted off the mouth of the Laerdal, along with steaming bowls of new potatoes and carrots and other vegetables. Sliced cucumbers and onions stood marinating in olive oil and vinegar. Fresh fruits were artfully piled on another platter. There were cheeses and pastries and fresh berries too, along with a goat cheese from Hallingdal.

"Did Denissoff ask you to bring him some wine?" Ritz asked puckishly. "He's always asking his visitors to bring wine."

"Yes," I nodded. "Some salmon flies too."

"Let me guess!" Ritz arched his expressive eyebrows. "Denissoff wants two cases of Piesporter Goldtröpfchen or Gewürzträminer — no that's probably wrong." He paused thoughtfully and frowned.

"You're close," I laughed. "Ockfener Bockstein."

"The old bandit hasn't changed!" Ritz ordered another bottle of wine. "He still likes those German and Alsatian wines."

"Want to venture a guess about the flies?" I asked.

"That's really too easy." Ritz swirled the fresh wine in his glass. "Denissoff uses nothing but a 5/0 Dusty Miller." He studied me with satisfaction and sampled the Chablis.

"You're right," I admitted.

Ritz approved the bottle of wine, and the worried Norwegian steward trembled as he filled our glasses. "Ernest," Ritz continued in a conspiratorial whisper. "You must understand about the Ockfener — you must make certain that Nicholas pays you for the wine!"

"But he's wealthy." I protested.

"No matter!" Ritz continued emphatically, while Creusevaut sat enjoying our conversation. "That's how he stays wealthy."

"Renting his river too," Creusevaut added.

Creusevaut and Ritz left for Oslo that afternoon, and their Caravelle flight back to Orly. Ritz rummaged briefly under their luggage to display a gargantuan salmon from the Årøy.

"Forty-six pounds!" Ritz announced proudly.

Since there was no available space for the Volvo on the Kaupanger ferry until evening, I decided to spend the afternoon with Olav Olsen, the famous fly dresser who lives at Laerdalsøyri.

Evening comes early in the Laerdal country, and its light lingers and dwindles imperceptibly until the fjord lies silvery purple. Several cars were waiting at the ferry slips. The night ferry across the Sognefjord sounded its arrival at Laerdalsøyri, its deep-throated horn echoing along the dark, mountain-walled sea.

Gulls hovered and screamed, wheeling above our ferry while the crew loaded our cars and the freight and mail on the landing. The trip takes almost an hour, crossing the smooth expanse of the fjord to Kaupanger. The passengers walked ashore, along with several cyclists who started up the long grade toward Sogndal. The night bus to Balestrand and the Jølstradal country rumbled off the ferry, and its passengers stood waiting on the quay. Finally the car deck cleared and I started the Volvo, turning it tightly to clear a starboard capstan. The car accelerated across the Kaupanger wharf, and I drove quickly into the forests toward Sogndal. When I reached the Danielsen pension, there was a brief message from Denissoff, instructing me to come at eleven o'clock for lunch at his fishing house.

*Tomorrow is really the day!* It was difficult to sleep with such anticipation. *Tomorrow we'll fish the Årøy!*

The entire fishable water on the Steeplechase measures less than a mile, although the river itself is three times that length. Its beginnings lie in the Hafslø lake, high in the mountains above the Sognefjord. Its outlet shallows are already a full-blown river, flowing swiftly over bedrock ledges, and measuring almost a hundred yards between its banks. Below those outlet ledges, the river drops into a wild series of staircase waterfalls and plunging rapids that fall 1,000 feet in less than four miles. The narrow cobblestone road winds above this torrent of tumbling water, switchbacking along the mountain until it reaches the fjord.

The Årøy Steeplechase lies just above the valley floor. Its upper beats lie at the bottom of this two-mile cataract, and their currents tumble swiftly in a final race to the sea. The river is enclosed in a sheltering little valley, embraced in its steep birch-covered hills and its mossy outcroppings of granite.

The Årven and Årøy farmsteads lie below the waterfalls that define the upper reaches of the Steeplechase, and the Denissoff fishing house stands across the river, high above the water and partially hidden in the trees. The famous casting platforms and weirs and tumbling rapids lie below the fishing house. Half-wild sheep forage on the hillsides. The masonry work bridge that crosses to the fishing house lies between these upper beats and the Sea Pool, which flows smoothly into the tidal shallows of the fjord. There are a few other buildings, along with a small power station above the fishing house, with a turbine that extracts electricity from the river.

Its currents race past the powerhouse, dropping into a swift, sickle-shaped mile of water and timber casting platforms. The river is a little frightening in early summer, even in its fishable reaches. The wild rapids that surge under the bridge drop almost 100 feet in the last 200 yards above tidewater. Wading such currents is impossible. The fishing is limited to bank-casting and the timber frames that were constructed after the First World War, casting structures that are called the Platforms of Despair.

*The currents are incredible!* Charles Ritz had explained in a letter from Paris. *There are casting platforms and artificial weirs in the river, placed to create spawning and holding-lies.*

These casting platforms and spawning weirs were originally planned and constructed by Major W.J. Smith, who had served in the Somme with the British Royal Engineers during the First World War. Smith had many years of experience on the river before that conflict, and often fished with the Duke of Westminster. His river structures were built in 1919, the same year that Smith killed a giant cockfish of fifty-four pounds on the Årøy Steeplechase.

*The wild torrents are the secret of the river*, Ritz continued in his letter. *The flow of the river is fierce, its bottom is filled with stones the size of oranges and cannonballs and grapefruit — and over thousands and thousands of years, only the strongest and largest fish could build their redds and spawn successfully.*

*Like other big-fish rivers*, I thought.

The wild character of the Årøy has shaped its unique strain of giant salmon. Its fish are unusually thick-bodied and deep, and the strength and spread of their tails are remarkable.

*Årøy fish average thirty-five pounds!* Ritz wrote.

Bigger salmon have been surprisingly common on the Årøy over the past century. Wilfred Kennedy took a fish of sixty-eight pounds on a prawn on the Sea Pool in 1894. Johannes Årven was the riverkeeper in the first years that Nicholas Denissoff held the river, and killed a monster of almost seventy pounds while fishing the Steeplechase alone in

1921. Denissoff killed three salmon over fifty pounds with a prawn that summer, including a huge cockfish from the Tender Pool that went seventy-six pounds. That prize is still enshrined in the museum at Bergen, almost matching the world-record salmon from the Tana in Arctic Norway, but most salmon fishermen revere the sixty-eight-pound fish that Denissoff took with his Dusty Miller from the Sea Pool in 1923. That trophy salmon is widely acknowledged as the world fly record, and a mural painting of the fish was lost when the Denissoff house burned in 1969.

"It's incredible fishing!" Ritz liked to explain in talking of the river. "It's like the Steeplechase at Auteuil!"

Nicholas Denissoff was an affable little man of puzzling origins, and there are several intriguing stories concerning the source of his wealth. It is known that Denissoff was born in Russia in 1883, and that his family was a minor pillar of the Russian nobility.

Following the bitter insurrections of workers and soldiers at Petrograd in the winter of 1917, other workers and dissident troops embroiled Moscow in the growing civil strife. Czar Nicholas attempted to put down these rebellions with a series of vicious reprisals in the streets. His elite horse-guards brutally decimated the marching strikers, and both Moscow and Petrograd erupted into brutal riots. Two weeks later, the besieged Czar was forced to abdicate, and the fateful struggle between various political and military factions began.

Lenin, Kerensky and Kornilov all attempted to consolidate their followers in new governments, and when Lenin failed in his attempt to seize Petrograd in the summer of 1917, it briefly appeared that Kerensky and Kornilov might forge a democracy in Russia.

Their coalition proved tragically weak and vacillating in the challenging weeks that followed. Kerensky refused to control or conciliate with Lenin and his militant colleagues. Chaos plagued the fledgling Kerensky government throughout its ephemeral rule. When the war with Germany went badly, promised social reforms failed to take shape, and the Russian economy tottered at the brink of collapse, the Kerensky government was clearly doomed.

Nicholas Denissoff found himself adrift in the crosscurrents of history, and his participation in these Byzantine intrigues was extensive. He was trained in both economics and civil engineering, probably in Germany and England before the First World War, and had played a major role in the construction of the Siberian Railroad. Its trackage totalled 4,500 miles when the final roadbed was completed at Lake Baikal in 1907. Denissoff and his family also held vast tracts of timber along the entire right-of-way according to many knowledgeable Russian exiles, and Denissoff served briefly as Minister of Finance to Czar Nicholas. Kerensky also sought his counsel in the troubled summer of 1917, but it was finally obvious that Kerensky and his government would fail.

The abortive fiscal condition of the Kerensky regime caused Denissoff to resign and liquidate his family holdings, travelling to London in the late summer to explore the sale of a privately held Russian banking house. Kerensky and Kornilov quarrelled bitterly while Denissoff was in London, and when Kornilov failed in his attempt to take Petrograd in September, the desperate Kerensky was forced to seek the cooperation and military support of Lenin, Stalin and Trotsky. When Lenin swiftly seized power in the bitter October Revolution, he forced the terrified Kerensky to flee, and Denissoff found himself stranded in the United Kingdom. Wild bloodshed and reprisals followed the collapse of the Kerensky coalition. When his entire family was butchered, Denissoff suddenly found himself the sole surviving partner of a private banking house in London. Most of his other friends and colleagues were also killed, or simply vanished into the wastes of eastern Russia. Other stories of his wealth argue that Denissoff had anticipated the collapse of the Kerensky government from its beginning, and had shipped a fortune in silver and family heirlooms and paintings to Zurich and Geneva. Perhaps each of these stories is true, since Denissoff held one of the most expensive fisheries in the world for almost a half century.

"The source of his wealth?" Charles Ritz concluded wryly over lunch at Laerdalsøyri. "Denissoff has the smell of intrigue!"

Ritz has described the Årøy Steeplechase with considerable detail in his *A Fly Fisher's Life*, particularly the excitement of his first meeting with Denissoff at Målangsfossen.

Denissoff and Popol Bernes, an old fishing comrade from

Switzerland that Ritz had known for many years, had been travelling together through Arctic Norway on a holiday trip to the North Cape. Denissoff promptly invited both Ritz and Jacques Chaume, his companion that week on the Målangsfossen beat, to join them for a fortnight on the Årøy. Ritz described that week of sport in *A Fly Fisher's Life*, calling it a wild mixture of impossible hopes, an almost crazy pitch of excitement, and a time of bitter depression and despair:

> *It was six-thirty when Jacques Chaume first threw his spoon into the Solkin Pool, which, with the Prawn Pool, is the best place on the river. At the fourth cast, he hooked a salmon. I went off to the platform where he was standing. Jacques was bending double and straightening up again, but could not succeed in stopping the fish, which was fighting like mad. Suddenly, his rod went straight. Broken! The nylon monofilament of .027 inches had been cut through on the rocks!*

Ritz continued with a description of the tackle in the equipment room of the Årøy fishing house. The rods were immense split-cane weapons from the craftsmen at Hardy and Farlow and Sharpes, some fashioned with steel cores, and a few of these colossal rods had been made by Asbjorn Hørgård at Trondheim. Several of these rods were as much as eighteen to twenty feet in length, and weighed between fifteen and twenty-five ounces. There were a few larger rods of spliced British manufacture that were shaped of Greenheart, rods that looked more like a medieval lance than fishing tackle, and Denissoff liked fishing them with a prawn. His fly chests were filled with traditional patterns dressed on huge 5/0 and 6/0 British irons.

There was a special tool that Denissoff had developed for braiding his heavy leaders, interweaving three strands of twenty-five-pound monofilament. His reels were big Hardy Perfects, their spools large enough to hold 200 yards of heavy squidding line for backing. Denissoff had lost many battles over the years, and he wrapped his fly knots with heavy silk and sealed them with fine varnish. Such equipment could only be described as awesome, and in the corner of the tackle room there was a broken gaff, its handle shaped from a discarded hoe. The gaff had shattered with the threshing of a giant salmon, fracturing the riverkeeper's hip when it escaped at Solkin.

Such armaments were often found wanting on the Arøy Steeplechase, like the parade of defeated anglers that had fished its Platforms of Despair. The outbuildings behind the fishing house concealed an elephant's graveyard of smashed rods and broken tackle. Ritz writes in his *A Fly Fisher's Life* that he lost nine immense salmon during his baptism on the Arøy. This passage describes his first hookup:

> *There was still a half hour of daylight. Perhaps I might have luck! And indeed, at the third attempt, I felt an appalling tug which nearly made me lose my equilibrium. I resisted the salmon with all my strength. The rod bent to its breaking point. I was trying vainly to recover line, when suddenly the rod snapped backwards, so quickly that I very nearly fell. I was broken too!*

Broken on a nylon monofilament of .027 inches, which had been carefully checked and tested. I was disconcerted, but had no regrets. To be soundly defeated by such a giant fish was honorable enough!

Denissoff confirmed such stories on the river during my week, including his own combat with a fish so strong that he fainted, and almost fell from the casting platform. His experience with these Arøy salmon had convinced him that the fish were unique, and those convictions have been echoed by others. Sampson Field described his adventures on the Steeplechase while we shared his beat on the Alta, and he spoke of the Arøy with a sense of awe.

"The currents are literally terrifying!" Field explained excitedly. "The fish can actually force you to your knees!"

Sampson Field hooked several of these monsters over the years, and many times the struggle became an ordeal. But the most frightening fish that Field saw hooked during his tenure of the Steeplechase took a big spoon off the Platform of Despair.

Field had fished through the holding currents first, and had finally surrendered the pool to Denissoff, who followed him with a heavy rod and a battered six-inch spoon. It was almost dark when the salmon stopped the fluttering lure, and it refused to move in spite of the straining rod or the tumbling rapids. Both Denissoff and Field were unable to move the fish, using all their strength until the braided leader throbbed and hummed in the current.

"It can't be a salmon!" Field shook his head unhappily and handed the rod to the old riverkeeper. "It's fouled on the rocks!"

Denissoff finally agreed that it was fouled and ordered the ghillie to break off the spoon while both men started back to the fishing house. Johannes Arven had fished the river since boyhood, and had killed a fish of almost seventy pounds in his youth. The keeper took the rod, walking the bank to change his position, and applied as much pressure as the straining bamboo could permit.

"Hjelpe!" the keeper screamed suddenly. "Hjelpe!"

Denissoff and Field came swiftly down the path, and were astonished to find the riverkeeper stumbling through the shallows, his face and arms bleeding as he fought the brush. Several times he fell among the rocks, tearing his boots and terribly scarring his legs. His hands had been badly lacerated on the line. Twice the monster salmon stopped in the churning torrents at the middle of the river, holding effortlessly against the sixteen-foot rod.

Suddenly the fish was running again, opening a terrible wound when the line burned across the riverkeeper's fingers, and the old man plunged back into the river. The lower casting platforms were ahead now, connecting the grassy banks with a marshy island where the Årøy gathers itself into the wild chute at the bridge.

It held there briefly, while the keeper fought to control the fight. The great fish shook its head in sullen anger, but the old river-keeper refused to surrender any more line, forcing the heavy steel-core rod into a frightening circle that threatened its life.

The salmon angrily wrenched out line in spite of the riverkeeper's strength, wheeled swiftly into the heaviest rapids, and cartwheeled clumsily just above the bridge. "It was unbelievable!" Field gestured with agitation. "I've caught several salmon over forty pounds in my life, and this fish dwarfed them — it was over seventy!"

The fish had broken the woven leader, and the steel-core bamboo was completely smashed through its butt. The men stood speechless on the casting platform, staring at the thundering chute where it had disappeared. Both Denissoff and his riverkeeper agreed that the salmon would have topped seventy pounds.

"It terrified me!" Field concluded sadly. "We walked back to the house without talking about the fish, sat down silently on the porch and consumed an entire bottle of Stolichnaya!"

The morning that my Årøy fishing started, I drove down past the farmstead at its mouth, where a small tree-covered island lies in the tidal flats. The fishing-house road drops down from the shoulder of the mountain to the narrow masonrywork bridge, climbing into the hayfields and birch groves beyond.

The Volvo was left in a clearing above the house, where two young ghillies were waiting to carry the wine, and I tucked the salmon flies into my shooting coat. The path wound across the meadow toward the house, where Denissoff stood waiting on the porch.

"Good morning," he called affably.

Denissoff seemed surprisingly small, dressed in a rumpled suit of British barleycorn tweed. His hacking boots were wet from the fresh dew along the river, and he studied his watch with satisfaction, since I had arrived precisely on time. Although he seemed frail, Denissoff was obviously wiry and strong for his eighty-three years. His thick little beard concealed his face, although it could not hide the brightness of his eyes. His English was surprisingly fluent, with faint echoes of the London years that followed the October Revolution, and his movements were unusually agile.

*He can't really be eighty-three!* I thought.

We shook hands like longtime friends, although there remained a touch of formality behind his gregarious small talk, and a serving girl brought us chilled vodka and caviar. Denissoff talked excitedly about his half century on the Årøy and the celebrities who had fished the river across the years.

"Before I took the lease fifty years ago," Denissoff explained, "the river was held by the Duke of Westminster."

"Didn't he fish the Alta too?" I asked in surprise.

"That's right," the old Russian nodded. "But he liked the Årøy for its seclusion as much as its giant fish!"

"Why was that?" I sampled his fresh caviar.

"Coco Chanel!" Denissoff laughed richly. "Coco was his lifelong mistress, and they often fished the Årøy together."

Chanel was justly famous for her classic clothing style, perhaps the finest couturier who ever lived. She lived for many years in the Hotel Ritz, occupying a tiny suite that overlooked the Place Vendôme, where she was legendary in her own lifetime. Charles Ritz managed the hotel from his elegant apartment across the hall. British society still talks of her liaison with the Duke of Westminster, although most people remember Chanel best for her costly perfumes.

"Westminster had excellent taste." I smiled.

"You're right!" Denissoff poured another pair of vodkas. "People in our valley tell me that he proposed marriage here."

"Proposed marriage to Coco?" I asked. "What happened?"

"She refused his proposal!" Denissoff explained puckishly. "Coco explained that history had already seen several titled wives who had married the Dukes of Westminster, and there would probably be more — but there would be only a single Coco Chanel!"

The serving girl returned to announce lunch, and we left the scrollwork porch. We stood waiting at the table while a young English nurse helped his wife to her place, and Denissoff hovered over them protectively until they were finally seated. His wife toyed strangely with her napkin, her slender fingernails clicking a curious rhythm against an empty wineglass. Denissoff smiled when he found me watching his wife, and poured me a little Piesporter.

"She's quite mad," he explained. "But she's happily mad."

The English nurse sat impassively through lunch, while Denissoff talked expansively and poured more wine, savoring its delicate tartness. "It was difficult to find the Ockfener in Oslo," I interjected, "but the Piesporter is fine too."

"It's quite good," Denissoff agreed.

When our lunch was finished and his wife had returned to her sitting room with the nurse, Denissoff conducted a brief tour of the house and its outbuildings. It was the main dining room that held a wall painting of the giant Denissoff salmon in the museum at Bergen, and another room was cluttered with cardboard tracings of other trophies captured over the years. There were literally stacks of these paperboard outlines that echoed fish over fifty pounds. The little workbench just inside the porch was mounted with the specially built machine that Denissoff used to braid his leaders, and the library cabinets held tray after tray of exquisite salmon flies.

"You must be christened!" Denissoff announced suddenly. "You cannot fish the Årøy until you have been christened!"

"Christened?" I asked. "What name will you give me?"

"Sascha!" Denissoff raised his glass.

Later we walked down from the porch to explore the casting platforms on the Steeplechase, while the young English nurse and her aging patient attempted an abortive game of belote in the parlor. Our first stop was the Platform of Despair, which lies just below the fishing house, and we walked upstream to the tumbling weir currents that frame Tender and the Home Pool. The main serpentine bridge crosses the river below the power station on the Årøy, its frightening maelstrom of currents churning through its pilings.

"Sascha!" Denissoff shouted a sharp warning about the rapids. "You cannot lean on the railings — they are merely for the psychology." The wild current roared past the planking under my boots.

"Thanks." I waved back weakly. "Thanks."

Denissoff stopped at various positions on the platform to point out casting stations and holding currents among the weirs. We finally crossed the river and I sighed gratefully in relief. Solkin and Prawn were downstream along that bank, and we sat down on the ghillie's bench.

"Ever lose a fisherman out there?" I asked jokingly.

"Never lost a fisherman," Denissoff replied with a wry smile. "But my river has drowned a few horses and pigs and cows!"

We walked slowly along the opposite bank, studying the swift lies below the groins and weirs downstream. Twice a huge salmon rolled off the lower platforms, where Denissoff and Field had lost the seventy-pound fish in earlier years. We crossed the bridge while Denissoff pointed down through the trees toward the Sea Pool.

"You will like that pool," Denissoff predicted confidently.

"Ritz liked it too," I nodded. "Why was that?"

"My salmon are so strong that Ritz lost every fish he hooked on his first trips," Denissoff replied. "Except in the Sea Pool."

"When can we fish it?" I asked. "It sounds good."

"First," Denissoff said, "we take a nap."

It was already late afternoon when I awakened on the porch, still drowsy with the mixture of vodka and lunch and wine, and my host came down a few minutes later. Denissoff stood buttoning his tweed waistcoat, his bright eyes dancing with anticipation. The old man explained his excitement with the observation that the tide had receded while we napped, leaving the Sea Pool at its optimum flow.

"The pool is quite beautiful," he said.

Denissoff was right, particularly with the shadows reaching across the water meadows and its casting platforms. The river tumbles from the birch forests below the bridge, dropping swiftly toward the salt-marsh tidewater downstream. The upper casting platform projects several yards into the current, and Denissoff explained that it fished well only when a high tide filled the lower reaches of the pool. The lower platform was yoke-shaped, reaching out through the sea-grass shallows into the principal holding-lies at low tide.

Eighty-five feet beyond the lower platform the wild currents of the Årøy Steeplechase were finally stilled, welled up smooth and silken in the afternoon light. Denissoff suggested that I rig my tackle, pointing out the primary taking places at midstream, but I wanted him to fish the Sea Pool while I watched. His ghillie readied a sixteen-foot Hardy, mounting a vintage Perfect with a mammoth agate line guard. Its woven three-strand leader was tipped with a 5/0 Dusty Miller.

"Petri beil!" I called from the bench.

Denissoff waved in reply and walked carefully along the casting platform, seeming almost as old as his years until he started fishing, but once his graceful Hardy was working eighty feet of fly line, his body looked lithe and surprisingly young.

Leaning back into another eighty-foot lift, Denissoff was

almost like a dancer as his line unrolled into a high backcast. The old man paused while the cast straightened, and drove back into his forward stroke like an athlete throwing his javelin. His line extended smoothly, dropping the fly ninety feet across the current. Denissoff placed the rod butt between his knees, gripped its butt section with the fierce concentration of a praying mantis. It was obvious that Denissoff understood each secret of the pool, and it took only a half dozen casts before his fly-swing stopped and he tightened into a fish.

"Salmon!" Denissoff cackled happily.

The heavy fish bored straight upstream, surged toward the surface and threw spray with its tail. Denissoff grunted and leaned backward into the straining sixteen-foot Hardy, its rubber butt cap firmly locked between his legs and both hands clamped around the butt guide. The fish stripped off staccato lengths of line as it probed high into the rapids, and the old Russian waited patiently.

*It's a good fish!* I thought.

Suddenly it tired of fighting both the river and the powerful split-cane rod, and it turned almost majestically toward the sea. Denissoff shouted gleefully when it jumped twice off his platform, writhing into its slow, pole-vaulting leaps that threshed water high on the wind. It was running again now, stripping line wildly into the fjord. When it broached far out into the tidewater, with almost a hundred yards of backing gone, the old Russian came running along the platform. Denissoff was shouting instructions, and the young ghillie plunged across the tidal shallows to launch the lapstrake skiff that was moored in the sea grass. Denissoff clambered into the boat, and the salmon was still taking line when they pushed off, stroking hard down the still expanse of the Sognefjord.

"Bon voyage!" Denissoff laughed. "Bon voyage!"

The fight lasted more than an hour. Several times they worked the big fish within fifty feet of their boat, only to have it strip line again in long reel-wearing runs. Finally it simply circled the skiff, straining hard to escape and too beaten to take more line. The ghillie started rowing back slowly, half towing the weakening fish, until they reached the small tree-covered island offshore.

Denissoff fought the salmon stubbornly, remaining in the

boat as the young ghillie slipped over the gunwales and walked it into the sea-grass shallows. The ghillie waded out with the gaff and waited, while Denissoff bullied the fish toward the beach. It finally surrendered, and the gaff went home in a tumultuous shower of spray. Denissoff quickly scuttled from the boat, while the huge fish came ashore fighting the gaff. The old man dispatched the fish with a stone, and they rowed back to the casting platform with the bright thirty-nine-pound henfish laid between the gunwales.

"Sascha!" Denissoff shouted. "Sic transit gloria!"

It was obvious that salmon fishing had lost none of its excitement for the old Russian, and his eyes glittered as the great fish was carried ashore. The old man followed the ghillie, showing no trace of fatigue from the fight. Although he held the world fly record for Atlantic salmon, and was eighty-three that summer, he still made each cast hoping for a bigger fish.

The following morning we fished the upper beats of the Steeplechase without success, working our flies through the churning salmon lies below the casting platforms. Although I was armed with a single-handed bamboo designed for fishing tarpon, when I finally hooked a fish at Solkin it proved so uncontrollable in the heavy current that I was almost relieved when the fly pulled out. We fished through the remaining lies of the Steeplechase without moving another fish, and finally drove down to the Sea Pool.

The tide had receded again, although the principal holding-lies were higher now, almost between the platforms. Denissoff pointed out the places where the currents welled up smooth and full of promise, like a cavalry officer planning his attack.

"The fish are lying farther upstream with this tide, and they're farther out," he explained. "Think you can reach them?"

"I'll try!" I was already stripping line.

It was slightly more than ninety feet, and I loaded the powerful Young parabolic with a hard left-hand haul and shot the entire line. Each successive fly-swing worked through the holding water as I teased it with the rod-tip rhythms. Several feet were retrieved before pickup, and I took a half step along the platform before making another duplicate cast. Covering a salmon pool properly is a mixture of precision and casting skill and patience.

"Sascha," Denissoff called jokingly from the bench. "You cast quite well but my salmon are ignoring you."

"They're pretty bored," I agreed.

There was a mammoth swirl that intercepted the fly-swing in the swift currents at midstream, and my rod bent double at the wrenching strike. The fish was simply an immense weight that ignored my pressure. It hung in the strong currents, sullen with its head-shaking anger as it brooded about its mistake. It refused to surrender line, and its spade-sized tail broke the surface angrily, throwing wild roostertails of water.

We saw the great fish clearly as it porpoised less than fifty feet beyond the platform. It shook itself again, its spray carrying downstream on the wind, and the fly came free.

"He's gone!" I shouted unhappily.

"Sixty-five pounds," Denissoff said drily. "You never really hooked him with that spaghetti rod you're fishing."

"Perhaps you're right," I said gloomily.

Later that week, Denissoff succeeded in taking a thirty-six-pound salmon in the swift currents of the Prawn Pool. It was the only fish that we landed from the Steeplechase itself, and its surprisingly brief struggle was an unusual fight.

Denissoff hooked the fish in the heavy flow just below the casting platform at the Prawn, locked the butt of his heavy Greenheart between his knees, and refused to surrender a millimeter of line. The salmon struggled and lunged against the powerful rod. It was simply a stubborn tug-of-war fight, lacking any overtones of skill or grace. The salmon fought with all its strength. It showered the old fisherman with spray, fighting in the swirling backwater under the platform. Denissoff cursed its strength in French and Russian.

Finally the fish weakened, and the young ghillie struck hard with the gaff, wrestling the salmon to the platform. "It's a fine salmon," Denissoff sighed. "But it's only average on my river."

"Thirty-six pounds!" I read on my Chatillon scale.

Our final lunch on the scrollwork porch was exquisite, sitting in the warm midday sun with the roaring of the Årøy Steeplechase in the valley below the house. Denissoff was a typically expansive mood, touching his beard with darting strokes of his napkin, and opening several perfectly chilled bottles of Ockfener.

His wife sat silently with a gently childlike smile, sometimes humming French nursery songs or toying absently with the tablecloth. The young English nurse sat quietly through lunch, stopping to help her patient drink some wine, and smiling faintly at Denissoff and his jokes. The cook usually prepared a cauliflower soup, or a rich consommé royale with a paper-thin slice of citrus fruit, but in honor of the first really hot afternoon of the summer, she had prepared a delicately spiced Vichyssoise.

"It's delicious!" I said happily.

The serving girl brought a succulent crown rack of lamb, its pink meat cooked to perfection, with tiny potatoes and vegetables and fresh mushrooms. There was a simple bean salad mixed with cucumbers before we were served the fresh fruit and Camembert. The coffee came with chocolate-covered *langues de chat*, and I declined when Denissoff offered a midday cognac with an excellent hand-rolled Habaña.

Although his boyhood Russia had been utterly destroyed in the bitter events that followed the October Revolution, there were still echoes of its world of elegant ballrooms and opera houses and glittering chandeliers in Denissoff's simple fishing house there on the Årøy.

"Are you tired?" Denissoff asked sleepily.

"Not tired enough to join you in a nap," I parried his suggestion. "Perhaps I'll try fishing the lower water again."

"It might fish well." Denissoff nodded and studied the clock above his tackle bench. "But the tide will still be pretty high."

"Should I fish it at high tide?" I asked.

"You should not fish the lower platform yet," Denissoff explained. "It fishes poorly until the tide has started ebbing, and we should not disturb it before evening."

Leaving the Volvo at the farmstead above the fjord, I walked down toward the Sea Pool. There was little current in the brackish eddies beyond the lower platform, although a single sea-bright fish rolled in its mixing tides, and it seemed a good omen.

The wild little Årøy dropped steeply from the bridge, slowing itself quickly in the eddying current tongues and tides beyond the upper casting structure. There were no fish showing there, but I fished it carefully several times, and fought the temptation to cover the main Sea Pool itself. It took almost an hour of patient casting to convince me that my luck was still sour, although a large fish rolled once and touched the fly. It refused to come again.

*Rest these fish a few minutes,* I though unhappily.

Resisting the lower platform again, in spite of the fish porpoising there steadily now, I stood watching the river in the late afternoon light. The tide had flooded high into the sea-grass border of the pool, and there was a brief flash as a fish rolled along the bottom. The fish flashed there again, catching the sunlight.

*It can't be a salmon!* I moved stealthily through the sea grass to get a better look. *There's too little current!*

Several fish were lying there in the shallows, slender and pewter-gray like salmon, although they seemed much smaller than the salmon we had taken. There were six fish lying together.

*Sea-run trout!* I though suddenly.

Quickly rigging a lighter nylon leader and tapering it with a series of carefully seated knots to a six-pound tippet, I selected a small Watson's Fancy from my fly book. It was relatively easy to align the school of fish with an outcropping of sea grass, and I returned to the casting platform to get the proper fly-swing. The first cast dropped above the fish, and I allowed it to sink deeply before a subtle Crosfield retrieve teased the drifting fly to life.

There was a bright flash over the pale bottom, and a strong pull that telegraphed back into the rod. When I tightened, the fish stripped line from the reel in a surprising run, taking sixty yards of backing before it stopped.

Patiently I worked it back through the tidal currents, where the mingling eddies were mixing now, signalling an ebbing in the Sea Pool. The fish stripped off backing again in another wild run, jumping twice before it came back stubbornly. bulldogging over the gravel in a series of head-shaking circles.

*Sea trout!* I thought with excitement.

The fat sea trout finally stopped fighting, and I coaxed it carefully into the shallows along the grass. It surrendered when

I seated my fingers across its gill covers, and I carried it gratefully ashore. The sea-run brown seemed huge, its coin-bright length measuring almost thirty inches, and I killed it mercifully.

The fished weighed nine pounds, and I walked back briskly toward the Årøy farmstead with its spotted tail dragging in the wild flowers. Denissoff had finished his nap when I reached the fishing house, and was sitting on the porch.

"Look at the sea trout!" I babbled with excitement. "You didn't tell me anything about big sea trout in the Årøy estuary."

Denissoff looked at the fish disdainfully.

"Sascha," he said with a fatherly sigh. "My river is filled with tigers and you waste your time with field mice!"

# Dean River Diary

## Ehor O. Boyanowsky

British Columbia is Canada's California of the mind, dominating the fantasies of its citizens in the way its sister state of mind far to the south did for Americans through many decades. I remember as a child sinking my teeth into a gloriously juicy Delicious apple during a frozen recess in the Northern Ontario sub-Arctic, and pondering the magical sort of place in which such a marvellous thing grew. If only one could get out to B.C.! One could get rich, live on a mountain, or by the sea, ski forever or sail over the horizon and catch fish on every cast — the possibilities seemed limited only by one's imagination.

Without the constraint of the seasons and traditions that are based entirely on the social order, a migrant fly fisherman arrives in B. C. and suddenly discovers he has died and gone to heaven! He can fish every day and almost anywhere — in streams, in creeks, in lakes, in the salt chuck. And this he proceeds to do, to the amusement, then bemusement, then consternation of family, employer and cleric. But just when his condition appears to be terminal and institutionalization by his worried family is in the works, he discovers *he is not alone.*

There exists, to provide social support for his condition, and legitimization for his deviant life style, a maniacal subculture within which he can immerse himself. This subculture casts an aura through which he can view "the rest of the world" (trans.:

time spent in places not fishing). Amazingly, access to this subculture is not based on having lived in a certain place for two hundred years, or having graduated from a certain college, nor is political affiliation a basis for membership. Rather, entry is based upon interest, skill and dedication. Why? Because these subcultures are spontaneously generated when isolates discover there are others like themselves around who love to be in one of the following altered states of consciousness: fishing, preparing to fish, talking about fishing, planning future fishing trips, tying flies or sitting through a three-hour-long session of fishing slides.

It was early in my condition that I bumped into Rick Jones on the Thompson River. Rick invited me to a meeting of the Osprey Fly Fishers — a club he headed as president, comprising a group of young Turks who true to West Coast fashion founded their own group when the "old club" was either booked up or unwilling to accept refugees of their stubble-chinned ilk. Oddly enough, I happened to be seated next to the guest speaker of that evening — odd because neither of us knew anyone in the club, and because he was a Totem: Jay Rowland. Jay, with his wry wit and a classic Runyonesque edge to his voice, was a fisherman of lifelong duration, who, according to his brother Scott, when he wasn't lifting little girls shirts in West Van, was poking around Brothers Creek with safety pin and willow branch, snagging cutthroat. One day relatively late in life, Jay had a mystical experience while watching a fly fisherman on the Stamp River and re-entered life a convert to the fly fishing faith. After that, he wasted little time devoutly visiting many storied fishing shrines of the American West, B.C., New Zealand and Alaska. At present he is, by the Waltonian calendar, an extremely precocious fourteen-year-old. Soon after that first evening, Jay called me up to go fishing and we visited the Cheakamus River. I remember it well, because it was one of those glorious shirt-sleeve-sunny January days and because I got my first speeding ticket in B.C. at Lonsdale Avenue, rushing to hook up with him.

In the absence of a non-fishing season the subculture marks the time of the year by the location of its 13th Tribe. This wandering elite are the Brahmin caste of the faith not just because they are exquisitely more expert, although practice surely makes perfect and some of them practice constantly, but because they have achieved the exalted state — they live to fish, and do so, effortlessly commandeering RV, boat, plane and sundry lackies to bear them to the appropriate shrine when it is in season. They are differentiated from mere mortals who appear only when they can get their holidays. And so, if this is the Morice and Tolley is here, it must be September. If this is Dragon and Anders is here, it must be October. If this is the Thompson and Wintle is here, it must be November. A handy calendar.

∫ ∫ ∫

The true Mecca, however, is the Dean River. A broad, jade-tinted stream, its lower thirty miles offers an exotic blend of mountain wilderness, luxurious reaches and deep pools, holding, when weather and season conspire to produce the right conditions, some of the brightest and most powerful, freely taking steelhead to be found anywhere. And the faithful assemble to pay them homage. A peculiar pilgrimage, because the primary goal is to do battle with these ghostly creatures, yet most often to return them to the river unharmed! It is at this juncture that one can distinguish the true meaningful difference between the western fly fisherman and his distant cousin back east, for a pilgrimage to the Restigouche is for the purpose of killing fish. To describe the return of a twenty pound fresh run steelhead to the river is to be met with stares of slack-jawed disbelief on the part of members of the eastern fraternity. They are, nevertheless, polite compared to non-fishermen who regard you with bald-faced cynical disdain and thereafter shoo their children away whenever you come into the room.

Every year, the Totem Fly Fishers mount an invasion of the Dean River complete with strategy-planning sessions, airborne raiding parties, advance scouts, armoured carriers, inflatable river craft and assault waves aimed toward various bivouac points. In retrospect it doesn't sound much like a holy pilgrimage, but then again, neither did the Crusades. The only guaranteed outcomes from all this effort are boundless good fellowship, priceless anecdotes and fond memories burnished to a soft glow by the firelight of passing winters. The fishing itself can be as uncertain as it is anywhere else.

To my delighted surprise, Jay asked one day whether I would be interested in coming along on one of these expeditions. He might as well have asked whether I wanted my Racquel Welch poster replaced by the genuine article. Of course there is an implicit danger to actualizing one's fantasies. Racquel could turn out to be the ultimate product of the prosthetician's art, but I was willing to take my chances with the actual Dean River. (On further reflection, I believe I could muster comparable courage at the prospect of Ms. Welch). This prompted a meeting with one of our party — David Elliott — also known in some circles (very small circles, I might add) as the Aluminum Coyote. He came over one day for a final briefing, very graciously bringing copies of the standard Dean River patterns for me to tie: Algan, Wintle's Western Wizard (pirated "Burlap" some veterans insist) Skunk, Deschutes Special, Skykomish Sunrise and the fabulous MacLeod Ugly — all tied on what appeared to me to be snaggers specials: gargantuan #2 hooks. In my uninitiated eyes they looked like the "joke flies" you see on the walls of riverside greasy spoons, and I sneaked a few sidelong glances to see if I was the butt of some joke on the greenhorn. But no one was laughing, so I accepted them gratefully and later in private tied a slew of sixes and eights and tens as I was accustomed to doing, occasionally producing a #4 and by girding my loins, at least one example of each in #2. Elliott was a type of phenomenon I had seldom encountered — with his meticulously cropped silver hair, his correct, slightly patronizing manner and impeccable general appearance, he dredged up memories of a coffin salesman who years ago had managed to make me feel guilty at the tender age of twenty-three for not investing in a family plot and elaborate King Tut type coffin. He quickly established that he was to be camp boss by producing a grocery list that in the intricacies of its calculations would have made Watson & Crick or any other biochemist blanch. I breathed a sigh of relief when I discovered he belonged to no evangelical faith and was even more comforted to discover this arcane formula was in reality translated into hauling off the shelves whatever caught one's fancy during the actual shopping. Dave was highly technical in many ways, having mastered the finer points of fly casting, tying, rod building and strategy to an amazing degree. Yet even with his irrepressible, almost evangelical, pedagogical bent, he managed to bite his tongue more often than not rather than lecturing me on my grotesque flies or wrap around casts (also requiring a high degree of technical expertise just to extricate oneself from). I did, however, learn a lot from watching him. In fact, countless trips to the interior, up the Indian Arm, lubricated by scotch on the rocks around the fly tying table and songs around the campfire on the Dean and at the International at Peter Hope Lake, mixed with reminiscences and trading of stories about ourselves, have brought us very close together. Closer than I ever dreamed possible when I surveyed the sea of strange faces across the table at the original Totems' meeting I attended.

Rounding out our group was Scott Rowland, Jay's brother, a free spirit who put fly fishing into perspective as an activity to fill one's time pleasurably in those moments between and perhaps when, one actually wanted to get away from the finer things in life. Scott enjoyed catching fish, but I have never seen anyone hang in there with greater good cheer than he did through six days of trials and tribulations without touching a steelhead.

In fact, that first trip put our values into perspective, for on almost any objective dimension it could have been judged to be the Dieppe raid of Canadian fly fishing campaigns. First, we feared a forest closure due to the long drought would force cancellation, but we got off. Second, after a breath-taking trip through the looming peaks and grey icefields of the coastal range, we clambered to the windows to get our first glimpse of the legendary Dean. Suddenly, it was below us and our hearts dropped — it was the colour of milk of magnesia!

"Looks fishable, not too bad," said Bob Taylor in his gentle, reassuring way. To me it didn't even look drinkable. We landed at Kimsquit in an Aero Commander. Through the sand storm of the sunbaked August drought we beheld a blue and red mass billowing out of the underbrush like an Arabian tent broken free of its traces. This form materialized over the shimmering dirt runway into the figure of a youthful lady of some generous proportions — the wife of the local caretaker and our sole source of transportation up the river — Twenty Dollar (make that $30) Felix. Ella's rather pleasant features were twisted by the agony of a messenger of ill tidings (since then we have discovered ill tidings are her specialty). The sad tale was that Felix's truck with its clutch destroyed, was stuck in a washout about a mile up the mountain. We set out after him with the afternoon sun hammering down upon us. Several pounds of sweat later we were pushing Felix's half-ton relic out of a massive washout, a foot at a go. Once out we freewheeled down the mountain praying his brakes would hold when they had to. Our prayers answered, we ended the day fishing the lower stretches among the bait flingers and spending the night in one of the abandoned cabins by the sea.

That evening Jay wrote himself into Ella's annals of infamy, for, when fetching water he dropped the bucket deeper into the well, not realizing it held Ella's chocolate pie, thereby destroying pie, polluting the well and destroying the seeds of what could have been a lifelong friendship. At that point we decided we'd better get up the mountain on foot early the next morning, while the getting was good.

∫ ∫ ∫

Elliott, ever resourceful, constructed a litter from our tent poles, tarp and oars using fiendishly clever knots, while we sneaked in "grannies" when he wasn't watching. Very soon we set out in the broiling heat. Halfway up the first leg, with sweat rolling down my body in freshet proportions, I mentally composed a letter to my Ukrainian father:

*Dear Father. This is "wacation" — paying two hundred dollars to fly to the Dean River and carry a hundred pounds up the mountain for miles in 90 degree heat, so I can sleep on the ground, get bitten by mosquitoes, chased by Grizzly bears and maybe catch a fish — that I throw back anyway. That is "wacation." Working is sitting by the pool in front of a typewriter with a gin and tonic watching girls in bikinis and getting a sun tan. Aren't you glad I got an education so I could take a long vacation and enjoy the finer things in life?*

It appeared as if we would have to carry Jay the last mile, but he managed to make it across the flood plain on his own. Once there, we discovered that a group of Americans had already taken the traditional camping spot on the Motel Run. We dropped our packs and collapsed in gasping heaps on the sandy shore, drinking thirstily under the sullen stares of this group of what appeared to be extras from the movie "Deliverance." Recovering our strength we waved hello to this surly cluster. None of them so much as twitched a whisker or spat a chaw of tobacco in our direction.

While we went back for a second load, Jay sought out another campsite, and finally we had a sort of camp set up — a blue flysheet stretched over a log with our sleeping bags laid out underneath.

Alas, the river had changed course and the Motel Run seemed no longer to hold great numbers of fish, so Dave and I decided to hike up to Four Mile where we'd heard Jerry Wintle, one of the gurus of steelheading, was camped. As we approached, we noticed a figure near the tent spot us, rise in leisurely fashion and purposefully, but unhurriedly, slide into the run.

"That'll be Jerry," said Dave. "It's eleven o'clock, he's probably just getting up. I'll follow him down."

I continued to the camp where a lady with a friendly smile and a snowy-haired gent who eyed me sceptically noted my arrival. The pleasant lady was Jean Wintle, Jerry's wife and fishing partner. The fellow was Martin Tolley — a noted B.C. fly fisherman who, according to Ed Weinstein, a friend of mine and a Stillaguamish regular, caused quite a stir on the Stilly many years ago as an apparition in deer stalker cap, tweed jacket and tie, wielding an outrageously large two-handed Spey rod. How far he has descended, I thought, in the grip of the savage colonies, standing there shirtless in the noonday sun. What was it they said about mad dogs . . . ? I inquired about the fishing, which had been unproductive, and whether anyone minded if I had a go?

"Oh, you can step in behind Jerry, or in front of him if you prefer," he said, regarding me with what I detected to be the hint of a supercilious smile. I elected to wait, and eventually Jerry came up to chat. This was the guy, according to my friend

Ed, who as a snotty-nosed new boy on the Stilly rendered the ace rod, Art Smith, near apoplectic.

"He caught steelhead in front of me, behind me, beside me! He's uncanny!" Smith apparently sputtered in the recounting later. Jerry allegedly exerted himself for neither man nor beast, rising near noon, using whatever flies were available, and casting with an air that was deceptively almost careless, belying its accurate, if unspectacular distance.

"Watch your fly box when Jerry's around," I'd been forewarned, but to the contrary, upon hearing that I'd recently arrived from the east and had never caught a summer-run, Jerry hauled out one of his own "Greaseliners," described how he and Harry Lemire had had a ball with it one day when the fish were rising readily, and told me to fish it straight across on a tight line into the white water. I did as I was told.

"Dobre!" Jean hailed from the shore, as I made my third cast mending immediately in the rough water. Just then a silver form swirled right in the foam and my reel howled as the steelhead hightailed it downstream towards Dave who ululated, and ran out of the run. Martin continued fishing. Puzzled, I called out to Dave, "What's the etiquette in this sort of situation?" which inspired only guffaws.

"You land the damn thing, that's what!" Elliott yelled back. By now the stream was vacated. Ten minutes later I was at the tail of the run with an eight-pound fish shimmering on the beach. The whole group gathered to admire my first summer-run, taken in classic style under the tutelage of the master, and with his fly.

Later, I learned that a perplexed Martin had come up to David after I entered the stream to inquire about the questionable sort of company he was keeping these days.

"Who is that hairy, hippie fellow, anyway?" asked Martin.

"Why he's Dr. Ehor Boyanowsky, associate professor of Criminology at Simon Fraser University," said David in his most grandiloquent, though tongue-in-cheek manner.

"Oh, oh," said Martin doing the classic, well-caned schoolboy's, reverent-to-authority about-face. "I think I've heard him on the CBC. He occasionally says something reasonable." Later as I chatted with Martin, watching his effortless casts to the current's seam, he inquired in a solicitous manner about the rod I was holding.

"A Winston graphite," I replied. "Would you like to try it?"

"No, thanks anyway," said Martin. "Rods built by white-coated women with computer-like precision hold little interest for me." And he turned with great dignity back to the stream to watch his white line unfurl gracefully against the dark current.

Eventually it became clear that the best holding water was at Six Mile, a long streamy pool marked by two flat cedar stumps situated in midstream at the head. Dave took a bright six-pound fish there on a floating line despite the opaque water, but between our American friends and the jet boats of the outfitters, no matter how early we rose, we were always stuck with the leavings, so we decided to camp over, right on the bar. We headed there in the evening before our last full day on the river and slept on the beach.

"I'll awaken you in the morning," purred Dave and so, comforted by his acceptance of responsibility, we dropped immediately into deep sleep. The next moment Dave was shaking me in the blue grey haze of the predawn.

"Wake up," said he, as I opened my eyes to behold him, fully decked out in waders, vest and cowboy hat, stepping deftly into the river.

"The sneaky sonovabitch!" the three of us chorused as we shook the fog from our brains. By the time we arose and donned our clothes and waders, Dave had fished through the whole run without a rise and had returned to shore to make the coffee. Jay went upstream to a little slot where he'd taken a fish once before. I covered the tail of the pool while Scott fished the head.

When I reached the bottom of the run, Dave called that the coffee was ready. I retorted that I usually like to fish another hundred feet down into the beginning of the white water. Two casts later my line stopped in midstream, I tightened, then cursed as I realized I must be snagged, but as happens too seldom, the snag started to move, then gathered speed. He ran down into the riffle and I chased him, then he stopped and sulked. Many minutes later, totally exasperated, we ended up throwing rocks at him.

"You've got a big Spring," Dave suggested cheerfully. But a ten minute tug-of-war finally revealed a stocky fourteen-pound steelhead buck exhausted on the beach. Jay had come up by then with a huge, shit-eating grin smeared across his face.

"How'd you do?" Dave could not resist asking, though his voice cracked.

"Two fish," Jay answered gleefully. "One a sixteen-pounder!"

Retribution, I thought quietly, exchanging smiles with Jay. By now even Scott's ebullience was somewhat deflated after five fishless days. So as time was running short, Jay suggested that just as an experiment, he try a spinning outfit. He then produced one from his knapsack with a matching rod. There followed an awesome display of deadliness. Within five or six casts, Scott hooked four or five fish and had a deliriously good time, hooting and shouting as he chased them down the run, the past gloomy days forgotten. A fresh wave of sports coming upstream for a week's fishing could hardly contain themselves, hollering, yahooing and waving their hats as Scott's fish cavorted before them. I pitied the guides. They'll probably be as easy to handle as a classroom full of hyperkinetic eight year olds, when they get to the lodge, I speculated. And so the trip ended much better than it began. We hiked to the road, where Felix picked us up in his newly-repaired truck and we coasted down to Kimsquit.

♪ ♪ ♪

Over the winter, with the fire crackling and ice cubes clinking in the scotch, we looked at the slides for the thirty-sixth run through. And we chatted about all the good times we'd managed to salvage from such potentially dire circumstances. It was clear we had to go back. Conditions had to improve, and perhaps we might even hit a bonanza of steelhead like Lee and Bob and Ham had. Scott wasn't keen, but we had a ready replacement in Ron Cordes. "The fabulous Ronaldo" Jay called him. We were curious to meet someone who had made an art of living the ultimate fly fisherman's gentle life. His J.D. in law and Ph.D. in engineering notwithstanding, Cordes was not your typical ulcer-ridden, achievement driven, upwardly mobile urbanite. He'd managed to spend no more than two and a half years of his whole adult life in gainful employment, yet lived in San Francisco, the most desirable of cities, drove a Porsche, not the least desirable of cars, and preferred to devote his energies to fishing, writing and the pursuit of feminine pulchritude at an unhurried pace across the face of the earth. Somewhere within this configuration we'd reckoned, there was a lesson in lifestyle (or at least in making it) to be learned. The Dean, in its remoteness, barring Ella and the occasional female grizzly, would prove a worthy challenge to his legendary extracurricular talents.

Curiously, Cordes turned out to be a very easy-going, quiet-spoken, somewhat reserved type who was a good companion, fine wit and an uncompetitive, but innovative fisherman. As it turned out, when groups of his compulsively friendly countrymen showed up to laugh and scratch, tell lies and consort with the near-great (Ron is on the staff of *Fly Fisherman* magazine) and the natives (us Canadians) he would, more often than not, quietly withdraw into the tent with a sci-fi novel.

It was August the 26th and we were the last wave of the Totem invasion for the year. There was one camp of four located at Twelve Mile, which we originally wanted but lost on the toss of a coin, and our own camp at Five Mile. As our plane rolled toward the oil drums in front of Felix's abode, Ella lumbered out of the underbrush, once again looking pained.

My God, I thought, It's déjà vu! What was it this time? Did she know Jay was in the aircraft and so she planned to roll a grenade our way before he had an opportunity to do his worst? Was the truck broken down? The road washed out in the monsoon we'd recently weathered after another drought? Was Felix hurt?

"The logging company won't let us travel the roads before five!" she informed us breathlessly. Oh no! But wait, maybe our luck had changed, as Felix was willing to drive the Five Mile group immediately and that was us!

What a pleasant change the camp was from the year before. Azure and orange fly sheets provided covered cooking and sitting areas, there was a table and log butts for chairs; best of all there was a wall tent, for the weather was cool and uncertain. I even spotted a rubber raft to ferry us across the river. My only concern was the three menacing deadfalls looming over the tent. Jerry Wintle came over to chat. The fishing was spotty, he related, but fish were showing up regularly. Most of all — the river was 50°F, low and clear and gorgeous! If I'm ever going to take another summer run on a dry fly, it should be on this trip, I thought, resolving to fish a floating fly for as long as I could hold out, even while my friends were derricking monsters out of the river on sunken flies to my right and left.

From our camp at Five Mile the river ran downhill in a long straight riffly pool — the one on which Lee, Bob and Ham did so well last year. Despite its productiveness, to me it looked bland; too much like a highway, though at the tail where it turned the corner, it became more appealing. Nevertheless, I was glad when Jay and Ron chose to cross in the raft and fish the other side. Dave and I hiked down to where the river poured through a series of small rapids into an intermediate pool with a classic throat and fan, then through many riffles into the fabled waters of Four Mile — a long, luxurious pool of slick water that moved about three miles per hour and went on forever.

We minced along in our Seal Dri waders. I was painfully aware of their reputed fragility, so I tried to avoid the tangles and devil's club. Dave started further down just around the corner below the Five Mile tail, fishing a MacLeod Ugly. I tied on a hugh #2 Miramichi Bomber, being now fully enured to the indelicacies of monster fly casting, and stepped into the river at last! Oh the exhilaration of fishing the Dean River again! Gloom clouded my vision as the cold chill of river water ran up my leg. Unbelievably, my virginal waders were punctured. I stumbled ashore muttering blackly to myself. What now! I tore off the waders, put on my wading boots and stepped back into the river. The icy waters clutched at my pant legs as I cast my fly. Inexplicably, the leader cracked like a .22 rifle. On my first cast, I had broken off my favourite fly. My eyes glazed with frustration, I tied on another, this time using the name for it more commonly preferred in less polite company, Fucking Ugly. I quartered a cast upstream, mended the line until the fly rounded the corner and kicked up a tiny rooster tail. Twice more I cast as I moved slowly downstream, my troubled mind calming somewhat to the rhythm of the casting. On the fourth cast, a silvery shape bulged at the fly, just before it turned the corner, starting me out of my reverie as it took off downstream cartwheeling repeatedly. Glory be! After my most inauspicious of starts, I was into my earliest fish ever. Obviously someone agreed that I'd paid my dues. But the fish was moving fast, churning downstream. I ran to head it off but it shot through the rapids below and kept going through the belly and toward the distant tail of Four Mile with me in hot pursuit. In the wider pool it chose to run to the other side and I finally got below her. Several runs later she was spent — length 32 ½", girth 16 ½", estimated at around twelve to fourteen pounds.

Dave looked at my fly, shaking his head.

Andy Anders, a genial retired airline pilot and a charter member of the tribe came over to inspect the fly. He too had been fishing wet. Shaking his head in disbelief at this deer hair version of one of the Muppets, he said, "It really is ugly, isn't it?"

Dave continued to fish through Four Mile. I rested, gathering my strength. Then I made a cast at the head. Surely it couldn't happen to me, I thought deliriously! A nice fish had risen and bumped the fly but didn't take. This was too much like a chapter out of Haig-Brown to be happening to me, but what the hell! I cast again as R. H-B recommended, and the fish took. Its eagerness notwithstanding, it was not an exceptional fighter, leaping twice in the pool, making two short runs then coming docilely back to the beach. I noted a bad seal bite on its shoulder. We returned to camp to learn Jay and Ron had hit none, but Jerry had hooked three, losing them all. Jerry noted ruefully that one fish had straightened the hook on my Muddler Minnow. One that I had seen him fondling in my box and so had offered to him in repayment for his Greaseliner of the previous year.

∫ ∫ ∫

The next morning Jay and Ron rode upstream with Felix to drift the river from Twelve Mile. Dave and I hit no fish across from the camp, but spent a pleasant time chatting with Dave

Winters who'd spent two weeks at Six Mile and had been into several fish. The fishing overall had not been exceptional, he related. We decided to walk up anyway, and have a look. The run had changed. The water was markedly lower, the stumps clearly protruding, the current was swifter at the tail and there was a well-defined lip before the white water began its downhill run.

Dave chose the head in front of the stumps. On my first pass below the lower stump, just off the gravel bar, a very large, powerful fish struck on a Black Irresistible given to me by Winters. It made one long, awesome run into the current. Inexplicably, I put a lot of pressure on it and the hook popped out. It was gone. Elliott slept on the bank awhile then stepped into the river above the first stump and was soon fast into a screamer that sped downstream and leapt below the second stump. His heart sank as it became clear his line was hooked on the stump, but we divested ourselves of cameras and waded into the chest-deep current. I held Dave by the braces as he swung out into the river performing an aquatic semi-pirouette that extricated his line. The fish immediately tore off a couple of hundred yards of backing. It appeared to be practically over the horizon when we last saw it leap. Dave stumbled along after it, banging a knee on the rocks, when, alas, it again became snagged on a submerged stump. Elliott appeared to be obsessed, he wanted the fish, which he estimated to be over twenty pounds, so we pussyfooted our way into the torrent arm in arm. Water was practically rooster-tailing over his back when we got to a stump above the critical one. I dug my toe into its rotten core and again swung Dave into the rapids by his braces like a sacrificial offering to the river. I wondered whether uninformed onlookers observing this spectacle would accuse me of intentionally drowning him if he slipped out of my grasp. All to no avail; he reeled the fish up almost to the snag, then the tippet snapped.

Jay and Ron drifted by. Jay, I noticed, looked like he had overdosed sucking lemons. Clearly, he hadn't taken a fish. Ron was more sanguine, having hooked one leaper and landed a coho for the pot.

The next morning Dave and Jay chose to fish Six Mile,

leaving Ron and me to fend with the assembled multitude at Four Mile. There was Andy Anders' crew, some six men strong, and Dave Kearney and Herb Spooner, two members of my own club, the Ospreys, who'd come in independently and were camped near the ranger cabin.

Jim and John, two of Andy's group, had spotted a good number of steelhead on the far bank some 100–130 feet distant. Ron had on his Hi-D shooting head along with his secret weapon — what he called a weighted fly, and we called a jig. He waded armpit deep and fired out this mini-killick. The river erupted as the largest steelhead I had seen on a line took the jig, leapt and popped it out, amazingly having straightened the forged hook! Immediately, he put on a Skunk and cast out again. Again he was fast to a big fish and once more it came off. The air crackled with anticipation. The weather was gloriously sunny and cool, the river was clear and obviously there was a good number of very large fish moving in the pool. Our gregarious American friends, veteran steelheaders as they were, pointed out how the steelhead spattered water on the surface; no bulge or roll, but a quick burst of thin spray, deceptively small for the size of the fish making it. This commotion signalled their recent arrival in the pool, and apparently their readiness to take.

I joined Ron, and in order to maximize my casting distance on the floating line, removed the bushy Greaseliner and put on a sleeker Davie St. Hooker — all fluorescent pink mylar, silver underbody and polar bear hair. My tenth cast stopped in midstream with an authoritative clunk and I was fast into a very heavy fish. Dave and Herb estimated it at more than seventeen pounds. When it broke water in the slow motion manner of large fish, at right angles to my line, it became clear that it was around a stump. Then it ran across the river coming unsnagged. Some minutes later, it began to tire and I pumped it shoreward. Unexpectedly, the leader suddenly broke at the second segment, near the butt. Obviously, it had been abraded on the snag. But a remarkable day, for I soon hooked another one of about twelve pounds that I chased through the rapids at the tail, managing to turn it into a backwater just before it ran into a log jam at the chute.

We had a singsong that night with Jay, Dave and me regaling

Andy Anders' gregarious group (in contrast to the American group of the past year) with our version of Staru Yushku (Old Mcdonald in Ukrainian), Mule Skinner Blues, The Wild Colonial Boy and others while some agent of the Devil in the employ of Jay Rowland lighted up our lives. Even Andy partook, though slack-jawed Jim squirmed on his piece of cordwood.

∫ ∫ ∫

We rose at 5:30 to beat the guide boats to Four Mile. They were clearly having trouble finding fish upriver as they were resorting to bringing their clients into the camper mob. The night had been warm and it was not unpleasant to rise in the gloom before sunrise. We arranged ourselves along the run. As the sun rose, Dave, who finally became a believer, put on a Greaseliner and was soon into a fish in the tail of the pool. It fought hard, leapt, then broke off. Half an hour later, I hooked one that ran down into the tail, heading into the same backwater before it broke off as I tried to haul it up the steep bank. Soon Ron was into a tremendous fighter, three-quarters of the way down the pool. It made several long powerful runs across the river interspersed with marvellous leaps before finally coming to the beach — his first Dean River fish, a very stocky, bright female. Only Jay who was fishing a Davie St. Hooker on a Hi-D head, had not touched a fish. Gratifyingly, we heard him call out soon after and watched as he chased a lusty twelve-pounder that alternately broke water and steamboated down the river. Moments later it too was on the beach — an absolutely gorgeous specimen. None of this group showed the seal bites or net marks of the earlier fish. I detected a smile; Jay had finally got the taste of lemons out of his mouth. We headed for camp, weary from lack of sleep, exhausted from the excitement, to perform our ablutions and doze away the afternoon. Even then thunder rolled across the peaks, and a heavy downpour began.

I awoke suddenly to the murmur of voices mixed with the hiss of the rain. Three wraith-like, dusky figures, drenched to the bone and smelling like polecats materialized at our tent door. They turned out to be the ubiquitous Martin Tolley,

Richard Thorpe, a British angling writer, and Bill Martin, a friend of Tolley's from Port Alice. I rose to put on a pot of tea and offered them some brandy. I always looked forward to seeing Martin. Inevitably there is an anecdote or two extracted from the interaction and I wasn't disappointed. They'd been drifting the river for two weeks with only a polyethylene sheet for shelter. It appeared to have been a very primitive enterprise.

"Quite a luxurious setup you have here," commented Martin. "One doesn't need all this to have a good trip though."

"Of course, Martin," I said teasingly, "but just because one is in the bush, one needn't live like a barbarian. Have some more brandy."

Ron and I wandered down to fish Four Mile, but the water was high and turbid. The sunset, however, was worth the trek. Later, we heard that Martin and Dave got onto the topic of rods, with Dave extolling the distance casting virtues of his new Golden West carbon fibre, built by Mike Maxwell, whom we'd met on the river the year before.

"Of course," asserted Martin, a traditionalist and, as you will recall, an exponent of the idiosyncratic charms of cane, "it isn't how far you can cast, but how the fly swims."

∫ ∫ ∫

Ron and I had been averaging a fish or two a day. Dave and Jay were, by contrast, not hitting many. By now, I had run out of Bombers and Greaseliners. Jay, munificent to a fault despite his slim pickings, gave me several examples of a creature tied with olive green deer hair and dubbing, that appeared part Greaseliner, part Muddler, part Porcupine. But it worked beautifully, so we called it the Rowland Hedgehog. One time, fishing Four Mile while Ron was chatting with, of all unlikely parties, a delectable young lady from Seattle named Mary Pritchard (clearly the Gods take care of their own), who was there with her father, I spotted a steelhead rising a mere thirty feet away. Stepping into shallower water, I covered it with a free drifting Hedgehog. Nothing happened. I decided to give it the textbook treatment for once. I tied on a smaller version in order to make twenty identical casts, then to move on, something I normally never have the patience to execute. Nothing stirred for thirteen casts. On the fourteenth, a steelhead inhaled it, hardly dimpling the surface!

Later, I stepped into the tail, drifting the Hedgehog through the riffle and had a steelhead boil at the fly. It did so again on six successive casts. By then I was practically beside myself with excitement and exasperation. On the eighth cast it too inhaled the fly. Again, there was no swirl or roll when it actually took, the fly merely disappeared, and again the fly was imbedded down in the gill rakers. Fortunately neither fly had touched the gills. Two fish that behaved like rainbow trout taking a dry fly — only they were giant rainbows, twelve pounds each! We called it a day. We returned to camp to find Jay keeping a stiff upper lip, but Dave was grinning like a Cairo rug merchant. And with good reason. He had struck a spate of fish in the tail of Six Mile, hooking five and landing four to thirteen pounds.

Jay wanted to go back to Six Mile on our last morning, and we just arrived there to have a jet boat pull in before us and drop an angler at the head of the run. Fuelled by the forty-five minute investment of energy required to trek there, the usually mild mannered Rowland went over to give this member of the jet set leisure class a piece of his mind. The angler, who very graciously stepped aside to give Jay first shot, turned out to be Joe Sladen, ironically, a former member of the Totems, and we ended up having a very pleasant time chatting. But no fish were taken, so we walked back to Four Mile where Dave was trying nobly to contain his glee. He had already landed three steelhead. Ron had lost two. By now we were all fishing dry flies exclusively.

Not surprisingly, the news did little to buck up Jay's spirits. But at least he appeared a bit diverted from his ill fortunes by the presence of Mary Pritchard who was spinfishing in the run near him. When she became snagged, he gallantly thrashed into the shallows to render aid. Taking the rod from her, he, unfortunately, immediately tripped the free spool lever, and line billowed from the reel like a macramé monster come alive. Mary sweetly asked for her reel, removed it from the rod, and cut out the line while Jay stood by sheepishly, mouthing pleasantries but not risking to offer further aid. As it turned out, she lost her spoon as well.

Soon after I stepped into the middle of the run and rose a fish. Jay wasted no time excusing himself from Mary and stepped in behind me. Three more times the fish rose without taking. By now Dave's exhilaration at his success was coming out in the form of rapid fire and exquisite criticisms aimed towards our suddenly loutish efforts to catch steelhead. We decided we preferred him less lucky and humbler. I moved down the run. It took Jay three casts to get to my former position. I had an ideal vantage point over my left shoulder as his Hedgehog swung by near me. One moment, I was admiring it, the next it vanished — again no bulge, no swirl — and perhaps the most beautiful steelhead we'd seen crashed through the surface into the air. A hard fifteen minutes later, we were inspecting it in the shallows. It was a glistening silver, fantastically spotted with an overcast of emerald green and with pink rays through the tail. A very unusual looking searun rainbow. Jay beamed quietly and went to sit on the beach. The river had finally come through for him in grand style.

The rest of us passed through the run several more times but only Dave took a fish — a powerful, very stocky female of about fourteen pounds. When you're hot you're hot. It proved to be the last fish of the trip, though I fished right through a blazing sunset well into the twilight, long after Jay and Dave had departed. I wanted a fish on the last day, but I could scarcely complain. Ron and I walked back to the camp in the gathering dusk, chatting quietly about this amazing river. A cold chill descended on the valley, a harbinger of autumn and the end of our season on the Dean.

# Fish are Such Liars

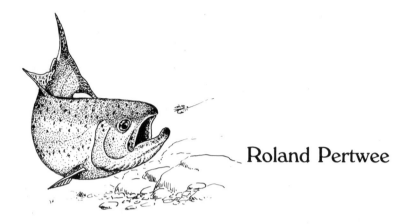

Roland Pertwee

There had been a fuss in the pool beneath the alders, and the small rainbow trout, with a skitter of his tail, flashed upstream, a hurt and angry fish. For three consecutive mornings he had taken the rise in that pool, and it injured his pride to be jostled from his drift just when the Mayfly was coming up in numbers. If his opponent had been a half-pounder like himself, he would have stayed and fought, but when an old hen fish weighing fully three pounds, with a mouth like a rat hole and a carnivorous, cannibalistic eye rises from the reed beds and occupies the place, flight is the only effective argument.

But Rainbow was very much provoked. He had chosen his place with care. Now the Mayfly was up, the little French chalk stream was full of rising fish, and he knew by experience that strangers are unpopular in that season. To do one's self justice during a hatch, one must find a place where the fly drifts nicely overhead with the run of the stream, and natural drifts are scarce even in a chalk stream. He was not content to leap at the fly like an hysterical youngster who measured his weight in ounces and his wits in milligrams. He had reached that time of life which demanded that he should feed off the surface by suction rather than exertion. No living thing is more particular about his table manners than a trout, and Rainbow was no exception.

"It's a sickening thing," he said to himself, "and a hard

shame." He added: "Get out of may way," to a couple of fat young chub with negroid mouths who were bubbling the surface in the silly, senseless fashion of their kind.

"Chub indeed!"

But even the chub had a home and he had none — and the life of a homeless river dweller is precarious.

"I will not and shall not be forced back to midstream," he said.

For, save at eventide or in very special circumstances, trout of personality do not frequent open water where they must compete for every insect with the wind, the lightning-swift sweep of swallows and martins and even the laborious pursuit of predatory dragonflies with their bronze wings and bodies like rods of colored glass. Even as he spoke he saw a three-ouncer leap at a dapping Mayfly which was scooped out of his jaws by a passing swallow. Rainbow heard the tiny click as the Mayfly's body cracked against the bird's beak. A single wing of yellowy gossamer floated downward and settled upon the water. Under the shelving banks to right and left, where the fly, discarding its nymph and still too damp for its virgin flight, drifted downstream, a dozen heavy trout were feeding thoughtfully and selectively.

"If only some angler would catch one of them, I might slip in and occupy the place before it gets known there's a vacancy."

But this uncharitable hope was not fulfilled, and with another whisk of his tail he propelled himself into the unknown waters upstream. A couple of strands of rusty barbed wire, relic of the War, spanned the shallows from bank to bank. Passing beneath them he came to a narrow reach shaded by willows, to the first of which was nailed a board bearing the words, *Pêche Reservée*. He had passed out of the communal into private water — water running languidly over manes of emerald weed between clumps of alder, willow herb, tall crimson sorrel and masses of yellow iris. Ahead, like an apple-green rampart, rose the wooded heights of a forest; on either side were flat meadows of yellowing hay. Overhead, the vast expanse of blue June sky was tufted with rambling clouds. "My scales!" said Rainbow. "Here's water!"

But it was vain to expect any of the best places in such a

reach would be vacant, and to avoid a recurrence of his unhappy encounter earlier in the morning, Rainbow continued his journey until he came to a spot where the river took one of those unaccountable right-angle bends which result in a pool, shallow on the one side, but slanting into deeps on the other. Above it was a water break, a swirl, smoothing, as it reached the pool, into a sleek, swift run, with an eddy which bore all the lighter floating things of the river over the calm surface of the little backwater, sheltered from above by a high shelving bank and a tangle of bramble and herb. Here in this backwater the twig, the broken reed, the leaf, the cork, the fly floated in suspended activity for a few instants until drawn back by invisible magnetism to the main current.

Rainbow paused in admiration. At the tail of the pool two sound fish were rising with regularity, but in the backwater beyond the eddy the surface was still and unbroken. Watching open-eyed, Rainbow saw not one but a dozen Mayflies, fat, juicy and damp from the nymph, drift in, pause and be carried away untouched. It was beyond the bounds of possibility that such a place could be vacant, but there was the evidence of his eyes to prove it; and nothing if not a trier, Rainbow darted across the stream and parked himself six inches below the water to await events.

It so happened that at the time of his arrival the hatch of fly was temporarily suspended, which gave Rainbow leisure to make a survey of his new abode. Beyond the eddy was a submerged snag — the branch of an apple tree borne there by heavy rains, water-logged, anchored and intricate — an excellent place to break an angler's line. The river bank on his right was riddled under water with old rat holes, than which there is no better sanctuary. Below him and to the left was a dense bed of weeds brushed flat by the flow of the stream.

"If it comes to the worst," said Rainbow, "a smart fish could do a get-away here with very little ingenuity, even from a cannibalistic old hen like — hullo!"

The exclamation was excited by the apparition of a gauzy shadow on the water, which is what a Mayfly seen from below looks like. Resisting a vulgar inclination to leap at it with the violence of a youngster, Rainbow backed into the correct position which would allow the stream to present the morsel, so to speak, upon a tray. Which it did — and scarcely a dimple on the surface to tell what had happened.

"Very nicely taken, if you will accept the praise of a complete stranger," said a low, soft voice, one inch behind his line of sight.

Without turning to see by whom he had been addressed, Rainbow flicked a yard upstream and came back with the current four feet away. In the spot he had occupied an instant before lay a great old trout of the most benign aspect, who could not have weighed less than four pounds.

"I beg your pardon," said Rainbow, "but I had no idea that anyone — that is, I just dropped in *en passant*, and, finding an empty house, I made so bold — "

"There is no occasion to apologize," said Old Trout seductively. "I did not come up from the bottom as early today as is my usual habit at this season. Yesterday's hatch was singularly bountiful and it is possible I did myself too liberally."

"Yes, but a gentleman of your weight and seniority can hardly fail to be offended at finding — "

"Not at all," Old Trout broke in. "I perceive you are a well-conducted fish who does not advertise his appetite in a loud and splashing fashion."

Overcome by the charm of Old Trout's manner and address, Rainbow reduced the distance separating them to a matter of inches.

"Then you do not want me to go?" he asked.

"On the contrary, dear young sir, stay by all means and take the rise. You are, I perceive, of the rainbow or, as they say here in France, of the *Arc en ciel* family. As a youngster I had the impression that I should turn out a rainbow, but events proved it was no more than the bloom, the natural sheen of youth."

"To speak the truth, sir," said Rainbow, "unless you had told me to the contrary, I would surely have thought you one of us."

Old Trout shook his tail. "You are wrong," he said. "I am from Dulverton, an English trout farm on the Exe, of which you will have heard. You are doubtless surprised to find an English fish in French waters."

"I am indeed," Rainbow replied, sucking in a passing Mayfly with such excellent good manners that it was hard to believe he was feeding. "Then you, sir," he added, "must know all about the habits of men."

"I may justly admit that I do," Old Trout agreed. "Apart from being hand-reared, I have in my twelve years of life studied the species in moods of activity, passivity, duplicity, and violence."

Rainbow remarked that such must doubtless have proved of invaluable service. It did not, however, explain the mystery of his presence on a French river.

"For, sir," he added, "Dulverton, as once I heard when enjoying 'A Chat about Rivers' delivered by a much travelled sea trout, is situated in the West of England, and without crossing the Channel I am unable to explain how you arrived here. Had you belonged to the salmon family, with which, sir, it is evident you have no connection, the explanation would be simple, but in the circumstances it baffles my understanding."

Old Trout waved one of his fins airily. "Yet cross the Channel I certainly did," said he, "and at a period in history which I venture to state will not readily be forgotten. It was during the War, my dear young friend, and I was brought in a can, in company with a hundred yearlings, to this river, or rather the upper reaches of this river, by a young officer who wished to further an entente between English and French fish even as the War was doing with the mankind of these two nations."

Old Trout sighed a couple of bubbles and arched his body this way and that.

"There was a gentleman and sportsman," he said. "A man who was acquainted with our people as I dare to say very few are acquainted. Had it ever been my lot to fall victim to a lover of the rod, I could have done so without regret to his. If you will take a look at my tail, you will observe that the letter *W* is perforated on the upper side. He presented me with this distinguishing mark before committing me, with his blessing, to the water."

"I have seldom seen a tail more becomingly decorated," said Rainbow. "But what happened to your benefactor?"

Old Trout's expression became infinitely sad. "If I could answer that," said he, "I were indeed a happy trout. For many weeks after he put me into the river I used to watch him in what little spare time he was able to obtain, casting a dry fly with the most exquisite precision and likeness to nature in all the likely pools and runs and eddies near his battery position. Oh, minnows! It was a pleasure to watch that man, even as it was his pleasure to watch us. His bravery too! I call to mind a dozen times when he fished unmoved and unstartled while bullets from machine guns were pecking at the waters like herons and thudding into the mud banks upon which he stood."

"An angler!" remarked Rainbow. "It would be no lie to say I like him the less on that account."

Old Trout became unexpectedly stern.

"Why so?" he retorted severely. "Have I not said he was also a gentleman and a sportsman? My officer was neither a pot hunter nor a beast of prey. He was a purist — a man who took delight in pitting his knowledge of nature against the subtlest and most suspicious intellectual forces of the wild. Are you so young as not yet to have learned the exquisite enjoyment of escaping disaster and avoiding error by the exercise of personal ingenuity? Pray, do not reply, for I would hate to think so hard a thing of any trout. We, as a race, exist by virtue of our brilliant intellectuality and hypersensitive selectivity. In waters where there are no pike and only an occasional otter, but for the machinations of men, where should we turn to school our wits? Danger is our mainstay, for I tell you, Rainbow, that trout are composed of two senses — appetite, which makes of us fools, and suspicion, which teaches us to be wise."

Greatly chastened not alone by what Old Trout had said but by the forensic quality of his speech, Rainbow rose short and put a promising Mayfly on the wing.

"I am glad to observe," said Old Trout, "that you are not without conscience."

"To tell the truth, sir," Rainbow replied apologetically, "my nerve this morning has been rudely shaken, but for which I should not have shown such want of good sportsmanship."

And with becoming brevity he told the tale of his eviction from the pool downstream. Old Trout listened gravely, only once moving, and that to absorb a small blue dun, an insect which he keenly relished.

"A regrettable affair," he admitted, "but as I have often observed, women, who are the gentlest creatures under water in adversity, are a thought lacking in moderation in times of abundance. They are apt to snatch."

"But for a turn of speed she would certainly have snatched me," said Rainbow.

"Very shocking," said Old Trout. "Cannibals are disgusting. They destroy the social amenities of the river. We fish have but little family life and should therefore aim to cultivate a freemasonry of good fellowship among ourselves. For my part, I am happy to line up with other well-conducted trout and content myself with what happens along my own particular drift. Pardon me!" he added, breasting Rainbow to one side. "I invited you to take the rise of Mayfly, but I must ask you to leave the duns alone." Then, fearing this remark might be construed to reflect adversely upon his hospitality, he proceeded: "I have a reason which I will explain later. For the moment we are discussing the circumstances that led to my presence in this river."

"To be sure — your officer. He never succeeded in deluding you with his skill?"

"That would have been impossible," said Old Trout, "for I had taken up a position under the far bank where he could only have reached me with a fly by wading in a part of the river which was in view of a German sniper."

"Wily!" Rainbow chuckled. "Cunning work, sir."

"Perhaps," Old Trout admitted, "although I have since reproached myself with cowardice. However, I was at the time a very small fish and a certain amount of nervousness is forgivable in the young."

At this gracious acknowledgement the rose-colored hue in Rainbow's rainbow increased noticeably — in short, he blushed.

"From where I lay," Old Trout went on, "I was able to observe the maneuvers of my officer and greatly profit thereby."

"But excuse me, sir," said Rainbow, "I have heard it said that an angler of the first class is invisible from the river."

"He is invisible to the fish he is trying to catch," Old Trout admitted, "but it must be obvious that he is not invisible to the fish who lie beside or below him. I would also remind you that during the War every tree, every scrap of vegetation, and every vestige of natural cover had been torn up, trampled down, razed. The river banks were as smooth as the top of your head. Even the buttercup, that very humorous flower that tangles up the back cast of so many industrious anglers, was absent. Those who fished on the Western Front had little help from nature."

Young Rainbow sighed, for, only a few days before, his tongue had been badly scratched by an artificial alder which had every appearance of reality.

"It would seem," he said, "that this war had its merits."

"My young friend," said Old Trout, "you never made a greater mistake. A desire on the part of our soldiery to vary a monotonous diet of bully beef and biscuit often drove them to resort to villainous methods of assault against our kind."

"Nets?" gasped Rainbow in horror.

"Worse than nets — bombs," Old Trout replied. "A small oval black thing called a Mills bomb, which the shameless fellows flung into deep pools."

"But surely the chances of being hit by such a — "

"You reveal a pathetic ignorance," said Old Trout. "There is no question of being hit. The wretched machine exploded under water and burst our people's insides or stunned us so that we floated dead to the surface. I well remember my officer coming upon such a group of marauders one evening — yes, and laying about him with his fists in defiance of King's Regulations and the Manual of Military Law. Two of them he seized by the collar and the pants and flung into the river. Spinning minnows, that was a sight worth seeing! 'You low swine,' I heard him say; 'you trash, you muck! Isn't there enough carnage without this sort of thing?' Afterward he sat on the bank with the two dripping men and talked to them for their souls' sake.

"'Look ahead, boys. Ask yourselves what are we fighting for? Decent homes to live in at peace with one another, fields to till and forests and rivers to give us a day's sport and fun. It's our rotten job to massacre each other, but, by gosh, don't let's massacre the harmless rest of nature as well. At least, let's give 'em a running chance. Boys, in the years ahead, when all the mess is cleared up, I look forward to coming back to this old spot, when there is alder growing by the banks, and willow herb and tall reeds and the drone of insects instead of the rumble of those guns. I don't want to come back to a dead river that I helped to kill, but to a river ringed with rising fish — some of whom were old comrades of the War.' He went on to tell of us hundred Dulverton trout that he had marked with the letter W. 'Give 'em their chance,' he said, 'and in the years to come those beggars will reward us a hundred times over. They'll give us a finer thrill and put up a cleaner fight than old Jerry ever contrived.' Those were emotional times, and though you may be reluctant to believe me, one of those two very wet men dripped water from his eyes as well as his clothing.

"'Many's the 'appy afternoon I've 'ad with a roach pole on Brentford Canal,' he sniffed, 'though I've never yet tried m' hand against a trout.' 'You shall do it now,' said my officer, and during the half hour that was left of daylight that dripping soldier had his first lesson in the most delicate art in the world. I can see them now — the clumsy, wet fellow, and my officer timing him, timing him — 'one and two, and one and two, and — ' The action of my officer's wrist with its persuasive flick was the prettiest thing I have ever seen."

"Did he carry out his intention and come back after the War?" Rainbow asked.

"I shall never know," Old Trout replied. "I do not even know if he survived it. There was a great battle — a German drive. For hours they shelled the river front, and many falling short exploded in our midst with terrible results. My own bank was torn to shreds and our people suffered. How they suffered! About noon the infantry came over — hordes in field gray. There were pontoons, rope bridges and hand-to-hand fights on both banks and even in the stream itself."

"And your officer?"

"I saw him once, before the water was stamped dense into liquid mud and dyed by the blood of men. He was in the thick of it, unarmed, and a German officer called on him to surrender. For answer he struck him in the face with a light cane. Ah, that wrist action! Then a shell burst, smothering the water with clods of fallen earth and other things."

"Then you never knew?"

"I never knew, although that night I searched among the dead. Next day I went downstream, for the water in that place was polluted with death. The bottom of the pool in which I had my place was choked with strange and mangled tenants that were not good to look upon. We trout are a clean people that will not readily abide in dirty houses. I am a Dulverton trout, where the water is filtered by the hills and runs cool over stones."

"And you have stayed here ever since?"

Old Trout shrugged a fin. "I have moved with the times. Choosing a place according to the needs of my weight."

"And you have never been caught, sir, by any other angler?"

"Am I not here?" Old Trout answered with dignity.

"Oh, quite, sir. I had only thought, perhaps, as a younger fish enthusiasm might have resulted to your disadvantage, but that, nevertheless, you had been returned."

"Returned! Returned!" echoed Old Trout. "Returned to the frying pan! Where on earth did you pick up that expression? We are in France, my young friend; we are not on the Test, the Itchen, or the Kennet. In this country it is not the practice of anglers to return anything, however miserable in size."

"But nowadays," Rainbow protested, "there are Englishmen and Americans on the river who show us more consideration."

"They may show you consideration," said Old Trout, "but I am of an importance that neither asks for nor expects it. Oblige me by being a little more discreet with your plurals. In the impossible event of my being deceived and caught, I should be introduced to a glass case with an appropriate background of rocks and weeds."

"But, sir, with respect, how can you be so confident of your unassailability?" Rainbow demanded, edging into position to accept an attractive Mayfly with yellow wings that was drifting downstream toward him.

"How?" Old Trout responded. "Because — " Then suddenly: "Leave it, you fool!"

Rainbow had just broken the surface when the warning came. The yellow-winged Mayfly was wrenched off the water with a wet squeak. A tangle of limp cast lapped itself round the upper branches of a willow far upstream and a raw voice exclaimed something venomous in French. By common consent the two fish went down.

"Well, really," expostulated Old Trout, "I hoped you were above that kind of thing! Nearly to fall victim to a downstream angler. It's a little too much! And think of the effect it will have on my prestige. Why, that incompetent fool will go about boasting that he rose me. Me!"

For some minutes Rainbow was too crestfallen even to apologize. At last:

"I am afraid," he said, "I was paying more heed to what you were saying than to my own conduct. I never expected to be fished from above. The fly was an uncommonly good imitation and it is a rare thing for a Frenchman to use Four-X gut."

"Rubbish," said Old Trout testily. "These are mere half-pound arguments. Four-X gut, when associated with a fourteen-stone shadow, should deceive nothing over two ounces. I saved your life, but it is all very provoking. If that is a sample of your general demeanor, it is improbable that you will ever reach a pound."

"At this season we are apt to be careless," Rainbow wailed. "And nowadays it is so hard, sir, to distinguish the artificial fly from the real."

"No one expects you to do so," was the answer, "but common prudence demands that you should pay some attention to the manner in which it is presented. A Mayfly does not hit the water with a splash, neither is it able to sustain itself in midstream against the current. Have you ever seen a natural insect leave a broadening wake of cutwater behind its tail? Never mind the fly, my dear boy, but watch the manner of its presentation. Failure to do that has cost many of our people their lives."

"You speak, sir," said Rainbow, a shade sulkily, "as though it were a disgrace for a trout ever to suffer defeat at the hands of an angler."

"Which indeed it is, save in exceptional circumstances," Old Trout answered. "I do not say that a perfect upstream cast from a well-concealed angler when the fly alights dry and cocked and dances at even speed with the current, may not deceive us to our fall. And I would be the last to say that a grasshopper skilfully dapped on the surface through the branches of an overhanging tree will not inevitably bring about our destruction. But I do most emphatically say that in such a spot as this, where the slightest defect in presentation is multiplied a hundredfold by the varying water speeds, a careless rise is unpardonable. There is only one spot — and that a matter of twelve yards downstream — from which a fly can be drifted over me with any semblance to nature. Even so, there is not one angler in a thousand who can make that cast with success, by reason of a willow which cramps the back cast and the manner on which these alders on our left sprawl across the pool."

Rainbow did not turn about to verify these statements because it is bad form for a trout to face downstream. He contented himself by replying, with a touch of acerbity:

"I should have thought, sir, with the feelings you expressed regarding sportsmanship, you would have found such a sanctuary too dull for your entertainment."

"Every remark you make serves to aggravate the impression of your ignorance," Old Trout replied. "Would you expect a trout of my intelligence to put myself in some place where I am exposed to the vulgar assaults of every amateur upon the bank? Of the green boy who lashes the water into foam, of the purblind peasant who slings his fly at me with a clod of earth or a tail of weed attached to the hook? In this place I invite attention from none but the best people — the expert, the purist."

"I understood you to say that there were none such in these parts," grumbled Rainbow.

"There are none who have succeeded in deceiving me," was the answer. "As a fact, for the last few days I have been vastly entranced by an angler who, by any standard, is deserving of praise. His presentation is flawless and the only fault I can detect in him is a tendency to overlook piscine psychology. He will be with us in a few minutes, since he knows it is my habit to lunch at noon."

"Pardon the interruption," said Rainbow, "but there is a gallant hatch of fly going down. I can hear your two neighbors at the tail of the pool rising steadily."

Old Trout assumed an indulgent air. "We will go up if you

wish," said he, "but you will be well advised to observe my counsel before taking the rise, because if my angler keeps his appointment you will most assuredly be *meuniered* before nightfall."

At this unpleasant prophecy Rainbow shivered. "Let us keep to weed," he suggested.

But Old Trout only laughed, so that bubbles from the river bed rose and burst upon the surface.

"Courage," said he; "it will be an opportunity for you to learn the finer points of the game. If you are nervous, lie nearer to the bank. The natural fly does not drift there so abundantly, but you will be secure from the artificial. Presently I will treat you to an exhibition of playing with death you will not fail to appreciate." He broke off and pointed with his eyes. "Over you and to the left."

Rainbow made a neat double rise and drifted back into line. "Very mellow," he said — "very mellow and choice. Never tasted better. May I ask, sir, what you meant by piscine psychology?"

"I imply that my angler does not appreciate the subtle possibilities of our intellect. Now, my officer concerned himself as vitally with what we were thinking as with what we were feeding upon. This fellow, secure in the knowledge that his presentation is well-nigh perfect, is content to offer me the same variety of flies day after day, irrespective of the fact that I have learned them all by heart. I have, however, adopted the practice of rising every now and then to encourage him."

"Rising? At an artificial fly? I never heard such temerity in all my life," gasped Rainbow.

Old Trout moved his body luxuriously. "I should have said, appearing to rise," he amended. "You may have noticed that I have exhibited a predilection for small duns in preference to the larger *Ephemeridae*. My procedure is as follows: I wait until a natural dun and his artificial Mayfly are drifting downstream with the smallest possible distance separating them. Then I rise and take the dun. Assuming I have risen to him, he strikes, misses, and is at once greatly flattered and greatly provoked. By this device I sometimes occupy his attention for over an hour and thus render a substantial service to others of my kind who would certainly have fallen victim to his skill."

"The river is greatly in your debt, sir," said Young Rainbow, with deliberate satire.

He knew by experience that fish as well as anglers are notorious liars, but the exploit his host recounted was a trifle too strong. Taking a side-long glance, he was surprised to see that Old Trout did not appear to have appreciated the subtle ridicule of his remark. The long, lithe body had become almost rigid and the great round eyes were focused upon the surface with an expression of fixed concentration.

Looking up Rainbow saw a small white-winged Mayfly with red legs and a body the color of straw swing out from the main stream and describe a slow circle over the calm surface above Old Trout's head. Scarcely an inch away a tiny blue dun, its wings folded as closely as the pages of a book, floated attendant. An upward rush, a sucking kerr-rop, and when the broken water had calmed, the dun had disappeared and the Mayfly was dancing away downstream.

"Well," said Old Trout, "how's that, my youthful skeptic? Pretty work, eh?"

"I saw nothing in it," was the impertinent reply. "There is not a trout on the river who could not have done likewise."

"Even when one of those two flies was artificial?" Old Trout queried tolerantly.

"But neither of them was artificial," Rainbow retorted. "Had it been so the angler would have struck. They always do."

"Of course he struck," Old Trout replied.

"But he didn't" Rainbow protested. "I saw the Mayfly go down with the current."

"My poor fish!" Old Trout replied. "Do you presume to suggest that I am unable to distinguish an artificial from a natural fly? Are you so blind that you failed to see the prismatic colors in the water from the paraffin in which the fly had been dipped? Here you are! Here it is again!"

Once more the white-winged insect drifted across the backwater, but this time there was no attendant dun.

"If that's a fake I'll eat my tail," said Rainbow.

"If you question my judgment," Old Trout answered, "you are at liberty to rise. I dare say, in spite of a shortage of brain, that you would eat comparatively well."

But Rainbow, in common with his kind, was not disposed to take chances.

"We may expect two or three more casts from this fly and then he will change it for a bigger. It is the same program every day without variation. How differently my officer would have acted. By now he would have discovered my little joke and turned the tables against me. Aye me, but some men will never learn! Your mental outfit, dear Rainbow, is singularly like a man's," he added. "It lacks elasticity."

Rainbow made no retort and was glad of his forbearance, for every word Old Trout had spoken was borne out by subsequent events. Four times the white-winged Mayfly described an arc over the backwater, but in the absence of duns Old Trout did not ride again. Then came a pause, during which, through a lull in the hatch, even the natural insect was absent from the river.

"He is changing his fly," said Old Trout, "but he will not float it until the hatch starts again. He is casting beautifully this morning and I hope circumstances will permit me to give him another rise."

"But suppose," said Rainbow breathlessly, "you played this game once too often and were foul hooked as a result?"

Old Trout expanded his gills broadly. "Why, then," he replied, "I should break him. Once round a limb of that submerged apple bough and the thing would be done. I should never allow myself to be caught and no angler could gather up the slack and haul me into midstream in time to prevent me reaching the bough. Stand by."

The shadow of a large, dark Mayfly floated cockily over the backwater and had almost returned to the main stream when a small iron-blue dun settled like a puff of thistledown in its wake.

The two insects were a foot nearer the fast water than the spot where Old Trout was accustomed to take the rise. But for the presence of a spectator, it is doubtful whether he would have done so, but Young Rainbow's want of appreciation had excited his vanity, and with a rolling swoop he swallowed the dun and bore it downward.

And then an amazing thing happened. Instead of drifting back to his place as was expected, Old Trout's head was jerked sideways by an invisible force. A thin translucent thread upcut the water's surface and tightened irresistibly. A second later Old Trout was fighting, fighting, fighting to reach the submerged apple bough with the full weight of the running water and the full strength of the finest Japanese gut strained against him.

Watching, wide-eyed and aghast, from one of the underwater rat holes into which he had hastily withdrawn, Rainbow saw the figure of a man rise out of a bed of irises downstream and scramble upon the bank. In his right hand, with the wrist well back, he held a light split-cane rod whose upper joint was curved to a half-circle. The man's left hand was detaching a collapsible landing net from the ring of his belt. Every attitude and movement was expressive of perfectly organized activity. His mouth was shut as tightly as a steel trap, but a light of happy excitement danced in his eyes.

"No, you don't my fellar," Rainbow heard him say. "No, you don't. I knew all about that apple bough before ever I put a fly over your pool. And the weed bed on the right," he added, as Old Trout made a sudden swerve half down and half across stream.

Tucking the net under his arm, the man whipped up the slack with a lightning-like action. The maneuver cost Old Trout dear, for when, despairing of reaching the weed and burrowing into it, he tried to regain his old position, he found himself six feet farther away from the apple bough than when the battle began.

Instinctively Old Trout knew it was useless to dash downstream, for a man who could take up slack with the speed his adversary had shown would profit by the expedient to come more quickly to terms with him. Besides, lower down there was broken water to knock the breath out of his lungs. Even where he lay straining and slugging this way and that, the water was pouring so fast into his open mouth as nearly to drown him. His only chance of effecting a smash was by a series of jumps, followed by quick dives. Once before, although he had not confessed it to Rainbow, Old Trout had saved his life by resorting to this expedient. It takes the strain off the line and returns it so quickly that even the finest gut is apt to sunder.

Meanwhile the man was slowly approaching, winding up as he came. Old Trout, boring in the depths, could hear the click of the check reel with increasing distinctness. Looking up, he saw that the cast was almost vertical above his head, which meant that the moment to make the attempt was at hand. The tension was appalling, for ever since the fight began his adversary had given him the butt unremittingly. Aware of his own weight and power, Old Trout was amazed that any tackle could stand the strain.

"Now's my time," he thought, and jumped.

It was no ordinary jump, but an aerial rush three feet out of the water, with a twist at its apex and a cutting lash of the tail designed to break the cast. But his adversary was no ordinary angler, and at the first hint of what was happening he dropped the point of the rod flush with the surface.

Once and once more Old Trout flung himself into the air, but after each attempt he found himself with diminishing strength and with less line to play with.

"It looks to me," said Rainbow mournfully, "as if my unhappy host will lose this battle and finish up in that glass case to which he was referring a few minutes ago." And greatly affected, he burrowed his nose in the mud and wondered, in the event of this dismal prophecy coming true, whether he would be able to take possession of the pool without molestation.

In consequence of these reflections he failed to witness the last phase of the battle, when, as will sometimes happen with big fish, all the fight went out of Old Trout, and rolling wearily over and over, he abandoned himself to the clinging embraces of the net. He never saw the big man proudly carry Old Trout back into the hayfield, where, before proceeding to remove the fly, he sat down beside a shallow dike and lit a cigarette and smiled largely. Then, with an affectionate and professional touch, he picked up Old Trout by the back of the neck, his forefinger and thumb sunk firmly in the gills.

"You're a fine fellar," he said, extracting the fly, "a good sportsman and a funny fish. You fooled me properly for three days, but I think you'll own I outwitted you in the end."

Rummaging in his creel for a small rod of hard wood that he carried for the purpose of administering the quietus, he became aware of something that arrested the action. Leaning forward, he started with open eyes at a tiny *W* perforated in the upper part of Old Trout's tail.

"Shades of the War! Dulverton!" he exclaimed. Then with a sudden warmth: "Old chap, old chap, is it really you? This is red-letter stuff. If you're not too far gone to take another lease on life, have it with me."

And with the tenderness of a woman, he slipped Old Trout into the dike and in a tremble of excitement hurried off to the *auberge* where the fishermen lodged, to tell a tale no one even pretended to believe.

For the best part of an hour Old Trout lay in the shallow waters of the dike before slowly cruising back to his own place beneath the over-hanging bank. The alarming experience through which he had passed had made him a shade forgetful, and he was not prepared for the sight of Young Rainbow rising steadily at the batch of fly.

"Pardon me, but a little more to your right," he said, with heavy courtesy.

"Diving otters!" cried Young Rainbow, leaping a foot clear of the water. "You, sir! You!"

"And why not?" Old Trout replied. "Your memory must be short if you have already forgotten that this is my place."

"Yes, but — " Rainbow began and stopped.

"You are referring to that little circus of a few minutes ago," said Old Trout. "Is it possible you failed to appreciate the significance of the affair? I knew at once it was my dear officer when he dropped the artificial dun behind the natural Mayfly. In the circumstances I could hardly do less than accept his invitation. Nothing is more delightful than a reunion of comrades of the war." He paused and added: "We had a charming talk, he and I, and I do not know which of us was the more affected. It is a tragedy that such friendship and such intellect as we share cannot exist in a common element."

And so great was his emotion that Old Trout dived and buried his head in the weeds. Whereby Rainbow did uncommonly well during the midday hatch.

# The Togariro

Zane Grey

Greatly to our satisfaction, we had a calm day for breaking camp on the Waihoro, and our run around the lake to Tokaanu. Once past the huge buttress of the western headland, we had full view of the beautiful Tongariro Mountain and beyond it the higher cone, Ngauruhoe, which shot aloft puffs of creamy smoke that mushroomed and hung in the sky.

As we neared the deep cut–in of the lake, where the red–roofed white houses of Tokaanu stood out clearly against the green, the high peaks dropped down behind Pihanga Mountain.

We passed the delta of the Great Tongariro River. The three mouths of the famous river had interested me for years. To one so given to imagination as I, the mouths of this river were disappointing. They ran over shallow sand bars into the lake. Captain Mitchell and I stood up on the deck of our launch the better to see. We ran quite close, expecting to have a good view of some anglers fly casting in the ripples; but all we saw were half a dozen skiffs, anchored at the several mouths of the river, and in each an angler sitting with an exceptionally long and heavy rod, and pulling his line in hand over hand. We had to wait a good time before one of them made a cast; but it was not a cast, just a fling of the line out, to let it float away with the current.

"By gad!" muttered Captain Mitchell. "That's the way they do it."

"Captain, it is not fly fishing," I said. "Most illuminating in regard to the heavy catches reported."

That alone decided us against camping at or near the delta. We had our outfit hauled up the river in a truck, and we went in cars to find a beautiful spot on a high bank, in a grove of trees, above the roaring rushing white and green Tongariro.

At last Captain Mitchell and I looked down into this trout stream, so celebrated among English anglers, and of which so much had been read by anglers of America. I could learn no word of any American ever having visited these waters.

"Shades of the Rogue River!" ejaculated the Captain.

"No, Cap, it's the green-white rushing Athabasca, which I wrote about in my story, *The Great Slave*," I replied.

Just to look at the Tongariro made us both happy. We could see bend after bend, pool after pool, rapid after rapid, all from the high bank at camp. There was a roaring rapid just above, not one of the deep-toned thundering falls peculiar to the Rogue, but a long narrow channel of white water, green at the edges, and just noisy enough not to be fearful. You did not think, "Suppose I should fall in there!" You just listened to the low murmuring roar. The Rogue, most wonderful of American trout streams, is a deep swift cold canyon-walled and rock-rapided river, hurrying down to the sea, with but few shallows and bars. The Tongariro appeared to have about the same volume of water, pale-green in color, exquisitely clear, too clear for fishing, and though a swift river, still it was not wild in its hurry to escape the confines of its banks. It was what I call a gravel river, there being bars and banks, all heavy gravel, and a river-bed of the same. In some places high banks of sand stood out of the green foliage, but for the most part the shores were sloping and covered with dense bush. Perhaps the most striking feature about the Tongariro in this section, six to ten miles above the delta, was the number and character of the islands. They were really gravel bars, under water when the river was in flood, and at low water picturesque green and gray islands around which the channels and rifts ran. Just below our camp the swift river broadened and slowed, with a wide sand and gravel beach on our side and a high bluff on the other, against which the current banked. From these points it separated into three channels, running in different directions, and dropped considerably to a lower level of the river. The channel that curved westward under our bank was narrow, shallow and boisterous. The middle channel took most of the river volume, and it roared down, deep and fast. The other channel ran glancing and smooth away to the southward, and dropped out of sight.

Our camp was situated in a grove of *ti* and *kowhai* trees. Behind the grove spread an oval green flat, dominated by two huge pine trees. Three poplar trees, also familiar reminders of my native land, stood up straight and tall, dressed in the gold of autumn, which contrasted beautifully with the surrounding bright greens. Far on the horizon rose the magnificent mountain range, wreathed at dawn by sun-flushed clouds, clear and sharp and dark at noonday, and at sunset half obscured in lilac haze.

It always takes time on new waters to find the best places and the right way to fish. Our Maori guide, Hoka Down, who owned the land round about, said the river was at the worst possible stage for fishing. A good hard rain was needed to start the trout running up from the lake. Still, he believed we might pick up a trout here and there, occasionally. I liked Hoka. He was jolly and fat, and he always wore a pleasant smile. He appeared well educated and sincere. He confided to Captain Mitchell his concern and regret regarding my visit to the Tongariro at a time when I would not get any of the wonderful fishing for which this river is noted all over the world.

The other side of the river looked by far the best, but we could not get across. We spent our first day crashing through the matted jungle of ferns and wading over the channels of the islands above. The water was so cold that it absolutely paralysed me through my waders. We built fires as we went along, waded and cast, and then splashed out to get warm. We tried an endless variety of flies. Captain Mitchell was partial to English flies — the Silver Doctor, Thunder and Lightning, Jock Scott, Sandy Special, etc. — and I pinned my faith as of old to the Rogue River flies. We did not raise any fish during the morning. Mr. Wiffin argued that in New Zealand sunshine was best for fishing. It had certainly been cloudy and dark, the very best kind of weather for trout fishing in the United States. Then about noon the sun did shine.

I put on one of the long light flies made from the checkered feathers of the bittern, and which had somewhat the motion of a little minnow in the water. I had used this with some success at the mouth of the Waihoro.

Casting this far out over the tail of a pool, where the water began to slide toward the rapid below, I let it swing around, and as it straightened out I had a good solid strike. Always that sensation will be electrifying. It elicited a shout from me.

"Hey, Cap! I'm fast to my first Tongariro rainbow!"

The trout did not show or leap, but he pulled hard enough to make me overestimate his weight. That proved to be six pounds. The rainbow trout never had his name more perfectly illustrated than in this colorful specimen.

We were encouraged to fish out the afternoon, working downstream and conquering obstacles in the way of dense thickets and slippery rocks. Late in the day I found myself at the pool just above the rapids which marked our camp. I chose the lower end, as seems always my way, and waded out to cast far across under the willows. I felt there must be a trout in the dark swirling water. So I cast and cast, all in vain; then, just to try to imitate Captain Mitchell in his everlasting patience and persistence, I kept on casting. The time came when I got a strike; a nibbling little tug! He had missed the hook. Whereupon I went on emulating Captain Mitchell. Soon I had another tug. This time I struck smartly. He was too quick. By now I had an audience in the shape of Morton, and Breckon, the expert photographer from the *Auckland Weekly*, both of whom had cameras ready. Thus encouragement was balanced against my exasperation, and I returned to my casting with more vim then ever. Then I had another touch. My line whipped up lightly, causing me to conclude the trout was a little fellow. Nevertheless I wanted more than ever to outwit him; and I cast with utmost care and precision, and with strung faculties. After perhaps as many as a dozen casts over the same place the trout rose for the fourth time, and I hooked him. To my amazement he felt solid, heavy, active. In one wrestling whirl he rid himself of the hook.

"By gosh!" I soliloquized. "Too slick for me! . . . And to think he fooled me into believing he was little."

Next morning we fished up a small stream that emptied into the Tongariro near camp. It appeared to be full of small trout, running up to three pounds. They rose to the fly, struck hard, and fought valiantly in the swift water. Several miles up this stream we came to a beautiful valley where the water ran level and quiet between banks of most luxuriant beauty. They were lined with the exquisite silver plumes, resembling pampas grass and known as *toi-toi*, and masses of bright green mint and watercress, yellow flowers, and clumps of low *ti* trees.

It was next to impossible to cast a fly over these verdant banks into the water. Yet we managed it occasionally; and when we got any kind of fly floating down the clear dark deep water near the watercress, there would be a swirl and a vicious tug. These rainbows were dark-backed and rosy-sided, some of them even gold in color. We lost many, and some we let go. Captain Mitchell lost six trout straight and the fact tickled me so that I conceived a vain notion that I would beat him this day, anyway. Nevertheless, though I started five ahead of him and kept going strong, in the end he forged ahead of me, catching twenty to my thirteen. Baker got five. There were many funny incidents, paramount of which was Captain Mitchell chasing some half-wild pigs. He had just landed a fine trout and laid it on the moss, when two pigs appeared. As he advised Baker to look out for one which went for his trout, the other pig seized Captain Mitchell's trout and ran off with it flopping from his mouth. The Captain gave chase. I heard the other fellows yelling, and turned in time to see Captain Mitchell running with all his might, and kicking the pig at every two jumps. His last kick hurt him vastly more than it did the pig, spraining a toe that had been injured during the war. The pig got away with the Captain's largest trout. The language our usually mild comrade indulged in was profoundly equal to any ever voiced by an angler.

We trudged home through brush almost as colorful and fragrant as my own purple sage, with a beautiful sunset in our faces, the mountains rising clear and grand on each side, and the melodious roar of Tongariro filling our ears.

"By Jove! What a perfect day!" exclaimed Alma Baker.

Hoka, our genial Maori guide, whom I had begun to like very well indeed, averred one morning that the trout had begun to run up the river, for he saw them. Both Captain Mitchell and I could verify this. To our delight and also exasperation we saw them too; but to make these rainbows rise to an ordinary fly was something which would tax the patience of a saint, not to mention a good degree of skill. The Captain did it, and so did I, but at the expense of infinite labor. We resorted to large Rogue River flies, mostly number four, and then to salmon flies number two, and finally we got to dressing our own flies. This was fun for me. Some of the outlandish lures I dressed up should have scared a rainbow trout out of his wits. Nevertheless they answered the purpose, and one of them, a fly so extraordinary that I could not make another like it, turned out to be a "killer." The only difficulty about large flies was that they were hard to cast. By diligent practice and strenuous effort, however, I at length achieved considerable distance, making an average of sixty feet, often seventy, and rarely even eighty feet.

We had word of another record catch of eleven fish at the mouth of the Tongariro. This was given us by Mr. Gilles, the mail driver, who stopped at our camp on an errand. He saw the fish and vouched for their weight; a fourteen-pound average, with largest weighing sixteen and one-half pounds. All caught on a fly at night! But no other information had been vouchsafed. I asked Mr. Gilles many questions about this remarkable catch, very few of which could he answer. He was himself a fisherman of long experience, a native of Tokaanu, and it was his opinion the trout were caught by the fisherman letting out a large fly or spinner a hundred or two hundred feet from the boat, and then drawing it back by hand until he had a strike. I shared this opinion.

By climbing to the bluff above the river, when the sun was high, we could see the big trout lying deep in the pale-green crystal water; ten, twelve and fifteen pound rainbows, and an occasional brown trout, huge and dark, upward of twenty pounds. This was a terrible, although glad experience for Captain Mitchell and me. To sight such wonderful fish and not get a rise from them! Alma Baker took it more philosophically, and considered the privilege of seeing them quite enough. Cap and I, however, wanted to feel one of those warriors at the end of a line. In the pool below camp we tried at sunrise, through the day, at sunset and then after dark. Fly fishing at night was an awful experience for me. I got snarled in the line. I continually hit my rod with my fly, and half the time it spun around the rod, entailing most patient labor. Moreover, I was standing through the chill of night in ice-cold water. Finally I whipped the big hook in the back of my coat. That gave me sufficient excuse to go back to camp. What joy the camp fire! Captain Mitchell returned presently, wet and shivering. He did not complain of the cold water, but he lamented a great deal over the loss of his best fly. He had snagged it on a rock and nearly drowned himself trying to rescue it.

Next morning while the rest of the party were at breakfast I stole down the bank and made a cast into the swirling waters. I made another, and when I strove to retrieve the line, lo! it was fast to something that moved. I struck, and I hooked a trout. For fear he might rush out into the swift current I held him harder than I would otherwise, and thus tired him out before he could take advantage of me. When I was sure of him, a fine seven-pounder rolling in the clear water, I yelled loudly. The whole breakfast contingent rushed pellmell to the bank, and to say they were amazed would be putting it mildly.

"By Jove!" ejaculated Baker. "You lucky devil! That's a fine fish."

"I wondered where you were," added Mitchell, with an experienced eye on my fish.

"You fellows have to have your tea, you know," I responded cheerfully.

That was a prelude to a strenuous day for all of us. Baker elected to fish the pools below camp, where he did not have to wade. Hoka took Captain Mitchell and me, accompanied by Morton, up the river.

"Only a little way, about a mile," said Hoka, with the smile that always robbed me of a retort. It was a long, long mile before we even got off the road; and even a short mile in heavy waders, three pairs of woollen socks, and iron-studded clumsy wading boots was always quite sufficient. I can pack a gun and walk light-footed far up and down canyons, but the wading paraphernalia burdens me down.

Hoka led us into a fern trail, one of those exasperating trails where the ferns hook your fishing line and leader and will not let go. Then he arrived at a precipitous bluff under which an unseen river roared musically. It was not the Tongariro. The Captain naturally wanted to know how we got down.

"We go right over," replied Hoka, and with the remark he disappeared. We heard crashings in the ferns. Next I went "right over." I held my rods high above my head and trusted my seven-league eight-ton boots to the depths. Then I went right over, but also down, my only concern being my rods. When at last I arrived at a comparative level, I awaited to see what would happen to my comrades. I knew there would be a fall all right. Soon I heard what might have been a rhinoceros plowing down the ferny cliff; but it was only Captain Mitchell, who arrived beside me hot, furious, forgetful of all save his precious pipe, which a tenacious fern still clung to. The real fun, however, came with Morton. Our genial cinematographer was burdened with cameras, also a pair of iron-hoofed boots that I had insisted he must wear. I have no idea how Morton got down, unless he fell all the way. We heard him talking vociferously to the obstructing ferns. At last he arrived, red of face, and grimly hanging on to his load.

"Dash it!" he panted. "You guys — must have had — persuaders to get down — that bally place."

The term "guys" Morton had learned from me and the word "persuaders" was a joke with us. While at our salt-water fishing on the coast I wrote about the teasers we trolled behind the boat, to attract swordfish. Whereupon an Englishman sent me a letter in which he said, "I note you use persuaders."

Hoka was waiting for us with his disarming smile. "You came down easy," he said. "But this panel over the river will be hard."

"Huh! What's a panel?" I asked. "Hoka, I've begun to have suspicions about you."

He soon showed us the panel. It was no less than a rickety pole bridge, swung on wires attached to branches of trees, and spanning a dark rushing little river that must have been beautiful at some other time. Just now it seemed a treacherous one. How the current swept on, down, down, rushing, swirling, gurgling under the dark over-reaching trees!

Hoka went first. He weighed seventeen stone, which in our language is over two hundred pounds; and I felt that if the panel held him it would certainly hold me. He crossed safely and quite quickly for so large a man. I went next. Such places rouse a combative spirit in me, and that made the crossing something different. Nevertheless when I was right in the middle, where the thin crooked poles bent under my heavy boots, I gazed down into the murky water with grim assurance of what might happen if the poles broke. I got across, proving how unnecessary the stirring of my imagination often is.

Once safe on the bank I was tempted to yell something facetious to Morton and Mitchell, but I desisted, for this was hardly the place for humor. They reached our side without mishap, and then again we beat into the jungle of ferns and *ti* trees. It was hard going, but soon I heard the mellow roar of the Tongariro, and with that growing louder and louder I found less concern about difficulties. We came at length into an open thicket of *ti* brush, bisected by shallow waterways and dry sandy spaces, through which we emerged to the wide boulder-strewn river bank.

"This pool here is called Dreadnaught," said Hoka, pointing to a huge steep bluff strikingly like the shape of a dismantled man-of-war. It stood up all alone. The surrounding banks were low and green. After one glance, I gave my attention to picking my steps among the boulders, while Hoka kept on talking. "My people once fought battles here. They had a *pa* on top of this bluff. I'll show you graves that are wearing away. The skulls roll down into the river. Yes, my people, the Maoris, were great fighters. They stood up face to face, and gave blow for blow, like men."

At last I found a seat on a log, laid aside my rods, camera and coat, and looked up. I was interested in the Dreadnaught Pool, of course, but as I did not expect to catch a trout I did not feel my usual eagerness and thrills. The Captain probably would land one, but the few preceding days and the condition of the river had dashed my hopes. So I seemed a sort of contented idle comrade, agreeably aware of the music of the river, of the westering sun, of the sweet open space all about me, and the dark mountain range beyond.

I espied Captain Mitchell, pipe in mouth, rod in hand, tramping over the boulders to the head of the pool.

"Hey, Cap, what're you going to do?" I shouted.

"Fuinshh!" replied the Captain, whom you could never understand when he had that black pipe in his mouth.

Thus I was brought back to the motive of this climb, slide, and plow up to Dreadnaught Pool.

The Tongariro ran sweeping down in an S shape, between bright soft green banks; a white swift river, with ample green water showing, and rapids enough to thrill one at the idea of shooting them in a Rogue River boat. Not a canoe, thank you! The end of the last rapids piled against the hull of the Dreadnaught bluff. A little rippling channel ran around to the right, out of sight, but it must soon have stopped, for the high embankment was certainly not an island.

I began to grow more than interested. The bluff had a bold bare face, composed of three strata; the lowest a dark lava studded thickly with boulders, the next and middle one a deep bank of almost golden sand, and the topmost a gray layer of pumice in the top of which I saw the empty graves of the bygone Maoris.

The current deflected from the base of the bluff, sheered away and swept down through the pool, farther and farther out, until it divided into three currents running into three channels.

The lower and larger end of that pool grew fascinating to me. Under the opposite bank the water looked deep and dark. A few amber-colored rocks showed at the closer edge of the current. It shoaled toward the wide part, with here and there a golden boulder gleaming far under the water. What a wonderful pool! It dawned on me suddenly. The right channel, or one farthest over, ran glidingly under the curving bank, and disappeared. I could not see the level below. Points of rock and bars of boulders jutted out from a luxuriantly foliaged island. The middle channel was a slow wide shallow ripple, running far down. A low bare gravel bar rose to the left, and stretched to where the third channel roared and thundered in a deep curving rapid. Here most of the river rushed on, a deep narrow chute, dropping one foot in every three feet, for over a hundred yards.

I had to walk to the head of the rapid to see where the water ran, heaping up waves higher and higher, down the narrow channel that curved away under another high wooded bluff. This indeed was a green-white thundering Athabaska. Most of the water of the pool glided into the channel, growing swift as it entered. Green crystal water! I could see the bottom as plainly as if the depth had been ten inches instead of ten feet. How marvellously clear and beautiful! Round rocks of amber and gold and mossy green lay imbedded closely, like a colorful tiling.

My gaze then wandered back over the head of the pool, where the Captain stood hip deep, casting far across into the current. And it wandered on down to the center, and then to the lower and wide part of the pool. What a magnificent place to fish! I made up swiftly for my laggard appreciation. I could see now how such a pool might reward a skilful far-casting angler, when the rainbows were running. After a long climb up rapids, what a pool to rest in! There might even be a trout resting there then. So I picked up my rod and strode down to the river.

A clean sand bar ran out thirty yards or more, shelving into deep green water. Here a gliding swirling current moved off to the center of the pool, and turned toward the glancing incline at the head of the narrow rapid. The second and heavier current worked farther across. By wading to the limit I imagined I might cast to the edge of that bed water. I meant to go leisurely and try the closer current first. It was my kind of a place. It kept growing upon me. I waded in to my knees, and cast half across this nearer current. My big fly sank and glided on. I followed it with my eye, and then gave it a slight jerky movement. Darker it became, and passed on out of my sight, where the light on the water made it impossible for me to see. I had scarcely forty feet of line out. It straightened below me, and then I whipped it back and cast again, taking a step or two farther on the sand bar.

Then I had a look at Captain Mitchell. He was standing

with that pose of incomparable expectancy and patience. No use for me to try to imitate him! The tilt of his old black pipe demonstrated his utter contentment. Well, I thought, I did not have any pipe, because I never smoked; but I felt that I was just as contented as he. Indeed I was not conscious of any other emotion. The fact that we were ahead of the running season for trout had operated to inhibit my usual thrill and excitement. It was the game to fish, to keep on trying, but I had not the slightest idea of raising a trout. If it had been otherwise I would have told Morton to be ready with a camera.

My line curved and straightened. Mechanically I pulled a yard or so off my reel, then drew perhaps twice as much back, holding it in loops in my left hand. Then I cast again, letting all the loose line go. It swept out, unrolled and alighted straight, with the fly striking gently. Was that not a fine cast? I felt gratified. "Pretty poor, I don't think," I soliloquized, and stole a glance upriver to see if the Captain had observed my beautiful cast. Apparently he did not know I was on the river. Then I looked quickly back at my fly.

It sank just at the edge of the light place on the water. I lost sight of it, but knew about where it floated. Suddenly right where I was looking on this glancing sunlit pool came a deep angry swirl. Simultaneously with this came a swift powerful pull, which ripped the line out of my left hand, and then jerked by rod down straight.

"Zee-ee!" shrieked my reel.

Then the water burst white, and a huge trout leaped in spasmodic action. He shot up, curved and black, his great jaws wide and sharp. I saw his spread tail quivering. Down he thumped, making splash and spray.

Then I seemed to do many things at once. I drew my rod up, despite the strain upon it; I backed toward the shore; I reeled frantically, for the trout ran upstream; I yelled for Morton and then for Captain Mitchell.

"Doc, he's a wolloper!" yelled the Captain.

"Oh, biggest trout I ever saw!" I returned wildly.

Once out of the water I ran up the beach toward Captain Mitchell, who was wading to meet me. I got even with my fish, and regained all but part of the bag in my line. What a weight!

I could scarcely hold the six-ounce rod erect. The tip bent far over, and wagged like a buggy whip.

"Look out when he turns!" called Mitchell.

When the fish struck the swift current, he leaped right before me. I saw him with vivid distinctness — the largest trout that I ever saw on line of mine — a dark bronze-backed and rose-sided male, terribly instinct with the ferocity and strength of self-preservation; black-spotted, big-finned, hook-nosed. I heard the heavy shuffle as he shook himself. Then he tumbled back.

"Now!" yelled Captain Mitchell, right behind me.

I knew. I was ready. The rainbow turned. Off like an arrow!

"Zee! Zee! Zee!" he took a hundred yards of line.

"Oh Morton! Morton! . . . *Camera!*" I shouted hoarsely, with every nerve in my body at supreme strain. What would his next jump be? After that run! I was all aquiver. He was as big as my big black Marlin. My tight line swept up to the surface as I have seen it sweep with so many fish. "He's coming out!" I yelled for Morton's benefit.

Then out he came magnificently. Straight up six feet, eight feet and over, a regular salmon leap he made, gleaming beautifully in the sun. What a picture! If only Morton got him with the camera I would not mind losing him, as surely I must lose him. Down he splashed. "*Zee!*" whizzed my line.

I heard Morton running over the boulders, and turned to see him making toward his camera. He had not been ready. What an incomparable opportunity lost! I always missed the greatest pictures! My impatience and disappointment vented themselves upon poor Morton, who looked as if he felt as badly as I. Then a hard jerk on my rod turned my gaze frantically back to the pool, just in time to see the great rainbow go down from another grand leap. With that he sheered round to the left, into the center of the wide swirl. I strode rapidly down the beach and into the water, winding my reel as fast as possible. How hard to hold that tip up and yet to recover line! My left arm ached, my right hand shook; for that matter, my legs shook also. I was hot and cold by turns. My throat seemed as tight as my line. Dry-mouthed, clogged in my lungs, with breast heaving, I strained every faculty to do what was right. Who ever said a trout could not stir an angler as greatly as a whale?

One sweep he made put my heart in my throat. It was toward the incline into the rapids. If he started down! But he ended with a leap, head upstream, and when he soused back he took another run, closer inshore toward me. Here I had to reel like a human windlass.

He was too fast; he got slack line, and to my dismay and panic he jumped on that slack line. My mind whirled, and the climax of my emotions hung upon that moment. Suddenly, tight jerked my line again. The hook had held. He was fairly close at hand, in good position, head upriver, and tiring. I waded out on the beach; and though he chugged and tugged and bored he never again got the line out over fifty feet. Sooner or later — it seemed both only a few moments and a long while — I worked him in over the sand bar, where in the crystal water I saw every move of his rose-red body. How I revelled in his beauty! Many times he stuck out his open jaws, cruel beaks, and gaped and snapped and gasped.

At length I slid him out upon the sand, and that moment my vaunted championship of the Oregon steelhead suffered an eclipse. The great Oregon rainbow, transplanted to the snow waters of the Tongariro, was superior in every way to his Oregon cousin, the silver-pink steelhead that had access to the sea. I never looked down upon such a magnificent game fish. No artist could have caught with his brush the shining flecked bronze, the deep red flush from jaw to tail, the amber and pearl. Perforce he would have been content to catch the grand graceful contour of body, the wolf-jawed head, the lines of fins and tail. He weighed eleven and one-half pounds.

As if by magic of nature the Dreadnaught Pool had been transformed. The something that was evermore about to happen to me in my fishing had happened there. There! The beautiful pool glimmered, shone, ran swiftly on, magnified in my sight. The sun was westering. It had lost its heat and glare. A shadow lay under the bluff. Only at the lower end did the sunlight make a light on the water, and it had changed. No longer hard to look upon!

I waded in up to my knees and began to cast with short line, gradually lengthening it, but now not leisurely, contentedly, dreamingly! My nerves were as keen as the edge of a blade.

Alert, quick, restrained, with all latent powers ready for instant demand, I watched my line sweep out and unroll, my leader straighten, and the big dark fly alight. What singularly pleasant sensations attended the whole procedure!

I knew I would raise another rainbow trout. That was the urge, wherefore the pool held more thrill and delight and stir for me. On the fifth cast, when the line in its sweep downstream had reached its limit, I had a strong vibrating strike. Like the first trout, this one hooked himself; and on his run he showed in a fine jump — a fish scarcely half as large as my first one. He ran out of the best fishing water, and eventually came over the sand bar, where I soon landed him, a white-and-rose fish, plump and solid, in the very best condition.

"Fresh-run trout," said Hoka. "They've just come up from the lake."

"By gad! then the run is on," returned Captain Mitchell with satisfaction.

I found myself out again on the sand bar, casting and recasting, gradually wading out until I was over my hips and could go no farther. At that I drew my breath sharply when I looked down. How deceiving that water! Another step would have carried me over my head. If the bottom had not been sandy I would not have dared trust myself there, for the edge of the current just caught me and tried to move me off my balance; but I was not to be caught unawares.

Sunlight still lay on the pool, yet cool and dark now, and waning. I fished the part of the pool where I had raised the two trout. It brought no rise. Then I essayed to reach across the gentler current, across the narrow dark still aisle beyond, to the edge of the strong current, sweeping out from the bluff. It was a long cast for me, with a heavy fly, eighty feet or more. How the amber water, the pale-green shadowy depths, the changing lights under the surface seemed to call to me, to assure me, to haunt with magical portent!

Apparently without effort, I cast my fly exactly where I wanted to. The current hungrily seized it, and as it floated out of my sight I gave my rod a gentle motion. Halfway between the cast and where the line would have straightened out below me, a rainbow gave a heavy and irresistible lunge. It was a strike that outdid my first. It almost unbalanced me. It dragged hard on the line I clutched in my left hand. I was as quick as the fish and let go just as he hooked himself. Then followed a run the like of which I did not deem possible for any fish short of a salmon or a Marlin. He took all my line except a quarter of an inch left on the spool. That brought him to the shallow water way across where the right-hand channel went down. He did not want that. Luckily for me, he turned to the left and rounded the lower edge of the pool. Here I got line back. Next he rushed across toward the head of the rapid. I could do nothing but hold on and pray.

Twenty yards above the smooth glancing incline he sprang aloft in so prodigious a leap that my usual ready shout of delight froze in my throat. Like a deer, in long bounds he covered the water, how far I dared not believe. The last rays of the setting sun flashed on this fish, showing it to be heavy and round and deep, of a wonderful pearly white tinted with pink. It had a small head which resembled that of a salmon. I had hooked a big female rainbow, fresh run from old Taupo, and if I had not known before that I had a battle on my hands I knew it on sight of the fish. Singularly indeed the females of these great rainbow trout are the hardest and fiercest fighters.

Fearing the swift water at the head of the rapid, I turned and plunged pellmell out to the beach and along it, holding my rod up as high as I could. I did not save any line, but I did not lose any, either. I ran clear to the end of the sandy beach where it verged on the boulders. A few paces farther on roared the river.

Then with a throbbing heart and indescribable feelings I faced the pool. There were one hundred and twenty-five yards of line out. The trout hung just above the rapid and there bored deep, to come up and thump on the surface. Inch by inch I lost line. She had her head upstream, but the current was drawing her toward the incline. I became desperate. Once over that fall she would escape. The old situation presented itself—break the fish off or hold it. With all that line off and most of it out of the water in plain sight, tight as a banjo string, I appeared to be at an overwhelming disadvantage. So I grasped the line in my left hand and held it. My six-ounce rod bowed and bent, then straightened and pointed. I felt its quivering vibration and I heard the slight singing of the tight line.

So there I held this stubborn female rainbow. Any part of my tackle or all of it might break, but not my spirit. How terribly hard it was not to weaken! Not to trust to luck! Not to release that tremendous strain!

The first few seconds were almost unendurable. They seemed an age. When would line or leader give way or the hook tear out? But nothing broke. I could hold the wonderful trout. Then as the moments passed I lost that tense agony of apprehension. I gained confidence. Unless the fish wheeled to race for the fall I would win. The chances were against such a move. Her head was up current, held by that rigid line. Soon the tremendous strain told. The rainbow came up, swirled and pounded and threshed on the surface. There was a time then when all old fears returned and augmented; but just as I was about to despair, the tension on rod and line relaxed. The trout swirled under and made upstream. This move I signalled with a shout, which was certainly echoed by my comrades, all lined up behind me, excited and gay and admonishing.

I walked down the beach, winding my reel fast, yet keeping the line taut. Thus I advanced fully a hundred yards. When I felt the enamelled silk come to my fingers, to slip on the reel, I gave another shout. Then again I backed up the beach, pulling the trout, though not too hard. At last she got into the slack shallow water over the wide sand bar.

Here began another phase of the fight, surely an anxious and grim one for me, with every move of that gorgeous fish as plain as if she had been in the air. What a dogged stubborn almost unbeatable fish on such tackle! Yet that light tackle was just the splendid thing for such a fight. Fair to the fish and calling to all I possessed of skill and judgment! It required endurance, too, for I had begun to tire. My left arm had a cramp and my winding hand was numb.

The fish made short hard runs out into the deeper water, yet each run I stopped eventually. Then they gave place to the thumping on the surface, the swirling breaks, the churning rolls, and the bulldog tug, tug, tug. The fight had long surpassed any I had ever had with a small fish. Even that of the ten-pound steelhead I hooked once in wild Deer Creek,

Washington! So strong and unconquerable was this rainbow that I was fully a quarter of an hour working her into the shallower part of the bar. Every time the deep silvery side flashed, I almost had heart-failure. This fish would go heavier than the eleven-and-a-half-pound male. I had long felt that in the line, in the rod; and now I saw it. There was a remarkable zest in this part of the contest.

"Work that plugger in close where the water is shallower," advised Captain Mitchell.

Indeed, I had wanted and tried to do that, for the twisting rolling fish might any instant tear out the hook. I held harder now, pulled harder. Many times I led or drew or dragged the trout close to shore, and each time saw the gleaming silver-and-pink shape plunge back into deeper water.

The little rod wore tenaciously on the rainbow, growing stronger, bending less, drawing easier.

After what seemed an interminable period there in this foot-deep water the battle ended abruptly with the bend of the rod drawing the fish head on to the wet sand. Captain Mitchell had waded in back of my quarry, suddenly to lean down and slide her far up on the beach.

"What a bally fine trout!" burst out Morton. "Look at it! Deep, fat, thick. It'll weigh fourteen."

"Oh no," I gasped, working over my numb and aching arms and hands.

"By gad! that's a wonderful trout!" added the Captain, most enthusiastically. "Why, it's like a salmon!"

Certainly I had never seen anything so beautiful in color, so magnificent in contour. It was mother-of-pearl tinged with exquisite pink. The dots were scarcely discernible, and the fullness of swelling graceful curve seemed to outdo nature itself. How the small thoroughbred salmon-like head contrasted with the huge iron-jawed fierce-eyed head of the male I had caught first! It was strange to see the broader tail of the female, the thicker mass of muscled body, the larger fins. Nature had endowed this progenitor of the species, at least for the spawning season, with greater strength, speed, endurance, spirit and life.

Then we left the rousing fire and strode off over the

boulders into the cool gathering twilight. Hoka carried two of my trout, Captain two, and Morton one. We threaded the *ti*-tree thicket and the jungle of ferns, and crossed the perilous panel in the dark, as if it had been a broad and safe bridge.

My comrades talked volubly on the way back to camp, but I was silent. I did not feel my heavy wet waders or my leaden boots. The afterglow of sunset lingered in the west, faint gold and red over the bold black range. I heard a late bird sing. The roar of the river floated up at intervals. Tongariro! What a strange beautiful high-sounding name! It suited the noble river and the mountain from which it sprang. Tongariro! It was calling me. It would call to me across the vast lanes and leagues of the Pacific. It would draw me back again. Beautiful green-white thundering Tongariro!